Some O

Copyrigh

Some Oth... ...

After consultation with contributors, a presumption is declared that all contributions contained within *'Some Other People's Lives'* have not been previously published commercially, and that no IPRs (Intellectual Property Rights) exist or are asserted by the contributors or any third parties at the time of publication.

This collection © 2015 Lawrence Milner & Dr. A. E. Richardson
Decade Publishing UK

Email: info.decadebooksuk@gmail.com

Jacket design by Lawrence Milner & Dr. A. E. Richardson, Copyright © 2015 Lawrence Milner & Dr. A. E. Richardson

Lawrence Milner & A. E. Richardson have asserted their right to be identified as the owners, compilers and editors of this work in accordance with the Copyright, Design and Patents Act 1998.

All rights reserved. No part of this publication may be reproduced, stored in a retrieval system, or transmitted in any form or by any means, including those of electronic, mechanical, photocopying and all recording systems, without the prior permission of the copyright owners

First published November 2015

V 1.0 November 2015

Opinions expressed in this work cannot be construed to represent those of the editors

ISBNs	*1519367104* / 978-1519367105
E-book ASIN	B018466NKC

Some Other People's Lives

Contents

Copyright & Disclaimer 1
Foreword.. 3
Slaying Dragons in London 5
Reflections on my Childhood - Alan's Early Years
1952 – 1973 28
The Diplo Cricket Match 50
Fly Fishing Idaho 57
Austrian Interlude 78
And a Rod for the Cat... 82
Train Spotting 95
Retyreing at Sea... 105
A Sporting Life 122
Thirty Three Years before the Mast with Narcotics
.... 140
It Started with a Kiss 153
United Brown States of America Road Trip 175
The One that Got Away.. 186
Spiritual Experiences.. 191
A Visit to a Star 197
Alan's Angling Adventures 207
An Offer of Marriage.. 229
Brushes with Death (A Painter's Story)................ 235

Foreword

"Future generations will wonder about us, but they will have very great difficulty knowing about us."

Vint Cerf, Google vice-president, Feb. 2015.

****

To adapt an extract from one of our great modern fiction writer's books, David Mitchell's *"Cloud Atlas"* :

"Our lives are as a drop in an ocean. But what is an ocean if not the sum of countless drops?"

Having made an astute observation that 'Ask Ron & Eddie' seemed like a cobbling together of individual stories of events and memories, my long-time friend, Dr. Alan E. Richardson, came up with a great idea:

"Why not invite our friends, families and contacts to contribute their stories to a 'short stories' book?"

Memories, he said? Very pertinent.

It is a consequence of the computer age that what we have actually come to refer to as 'memory', recollections if you like, is perceived not as the 'data' or actual memories, but the empty medium (a memory card, floppy disc or iCloud etc.) in which 'memories' (data, stories, events) are stored. In modern parlance, therefore, memory may now be more accurately defined as a 'rememberer', a device of one sort or another which stores and facilitates the retrieval and promulgation of 'data'.

Like a computer without a hard drive or memory card, like an iPhone without the 'iCloud' perhaps, this 'data', these stories, these memories of events, our memories and yours, may inevitably no longer exist as such without a host, a 'rememberer', to store (remember), recall and communicate them.

So is it fair to say that there can be no data, no 'memory' of stories and events, without a rememberer? We think so.

Sadly, there must be so many tales of our long-gone friends' and families' lives that may have been told, but have now vanished, evaporated into the ether. Unless one can record or store 'events' to a rememberer, and so enable their promulgation, communication, recollection, recounting and sharing, if you will, with other 'rememberers', they will eventually be lost forever.

Of course a rememberer could equally be a book, a piece of paper, or a Kindle eBook Reader or similar device, and so the concept of *"Some Other People's Lives"* came into being, where we mere 'drops in the ocean' can take the opportunity to enable our stories to be shared by other rememberers, to 'make our mark' if you like, our stories being further acknowledged and remembered in this ocean of humankind.

Thanks must go to all those who contributed their 'drops in the ocean' stories, and so made them available to us. Thanks may also need to be tendered to our families, certainly to Alan's and mine, for temporarily losing us in our obsession with facilitating the sharing of these stories from Some Other People's Lives.

We hope you enjoy them.

Lawrence Milner & Dr. A. E. Richardson

Slaying Dragons in London
by Michele Phillips Copp, USA

In 1986 I was 25 and had recently started my first career job after university, but I had an addiction – an addiction to England and all things English. This addiction had started many years earlier and escalated when, in 1974, I discovered the Beatles and became obsessed with them. It intensified further when Lady Di (the future Princess Diana) came on the scene.

My best friend also suffered from the same addiction, and two years earlier Gloria and I had scrimped and saved for nine months to fund a three week trip to our beloved England. Alas, like most addictions, getting a fix intensifies the cravings. A year later, with far less funds, we returned, but had to limit ourselves to a mere seven days this time.

The day I returned home, I immediately started saving (while still working on my Accounting degree) for the next trip. Unfortunately, Gloria was not able to travel that year. This left me in a bind. I had no other friends who were willing and able to go leading me to make an uncharacteristic decision – I would go alone. That solo trip proved to be a little bit of a disaster as I had a panic attack the day I arrived and ended dramatically with many tears and returning home a week later with my tail between my legs.

They say the best way to recover from a mishap is to get back up on that horse as soon as possible. So the next year I went again, but this time I took my cousin Kelly with me. She was six years younger than me and lived hundreds of miles away from me, but through letter writing and phone calls we'd become like sisters.

It is here that I also have to confess that I actually had two addictions by now. For years I had a huge portfolio of pen friends around the world. The number varied but at my all-time high I was writing to twenty people around the world including my cousin Kelly. However, a handful of these pen friends lived scattered around England and one in particular had become very special to me.

Ernie, my other addiction, conveniently lived in a London suburb called Croydon and he'd shown us a lovely time when we visited him on my previous trips. I wasn't sure he felt the same as me, but the odds were good. We wrote to each other more frequently than any of the other pen friends did and he always wrote lovely letters full of information about his daily life. He sent me valentines and gifts and I was smitten.

That trip with Kelly was magical. Not only did I travel without any of the anxiety and panic of the previous year, but Ernie outdid himself to show us a good time. He took us on day trips to Henley-on-Thames and Liverpool and even brought his younger cousin David along so that Kelly had someone closer to her own age to chat with.

So when that trip was over, the routine continued. I wanted to return as always. But Kelly couldn't go. Gloria couldn't go. I again found myself in the scary predicament of being able to afford to the trip, but facing the prospect of going alone again. This brought all the memories of that awful panic attack flooding back and I had to think long and hard about it.

Addictions by their very nature cause us to do things we know we shouldn't and the draw of London, and seeing Ernie again were too strong; I made the decision to go. However, I was older now (a whole two years older) and more mature (I told myself). I analyzed that disaster trip to identify what had caused the panic. I realized that I had relied too much on the assumption that things would be the same and when things weren't the same and minor problems arose, I didn't handle the changes well and fell apart.

So I made a list of the things that had upset me and worked on ways to give me more control.

In the disaster trip from two years earlier, I had booked into the same B&B I'd stayed in the previous year in a double room with Gloria. That lovely room had been close to the bathroom and hall phone and was large and airy and just one floor away from the lobby. The following year, as a single traveler, I was put in an miniscule attic room, four flights up from the lobby and six flights up from the phone. The bathroom was not that nice and didn't work well. So I knew I needed to spend a bit more to make sure I had a room I would be happy in. I decided to book into the same hotel that Kelly and I had just stayed in and pay extra to have my own private bathroom. The room and the neighborhood would be familiar which would also help. I even specified in my reservation request that I wanted a room with a view.

I had also panicked on the disaster trip when I was unable to reach Ernie due to telephone switch problems. I was in the country three days before I was able to speak to him, and it really would have helped to be able to talk to him sooner. To solve this problem, I wrote to Ernie and he agreed to set up our first meet up in advance, so that even if all the phones were broken, I would know how to find him. We agreed to meet for dinner on my second night at the Angus Steak House in Baker Street near his work.

My analysis also showed it would have been a good idea to plan out my first few days so that I didn't have to try to plan while anxious. I had discovered that when panicked, being faced with two dozen index cards of possibilities was overwhelming. So, I made a plan and detailed exactly how I would spend my first two days in London. I decided what I would see or visit and when and where I would eat my meals. It sounds too scripted, but I knew if I wanted to I could throw out the plan, but if I needed it, it would be my crutch.

With my strategy in place, I took a leap of faith and booked a three week trip to London on my own - again. The one thing that was different was the time of year. All my previous trips had been in summer between semesters. Now that I had started my new job, I had to wait until October. This was one variable I couldn't help.

The days sped by and before I knew it, it was time to leave for the airport. As my mom and dad dropped me off at the airport, my dad gave me a hug. I don't come from a family of huggers. Already nervous and edgy, this started the tears flowing as I hugged him back. I know we were both remembering my frantic call to his office two years earlier when I sobbed that I wanted to come home just hours after landing.

"Are you sure you are OK and want to do this?" Dad asked?

"Yes," I blubbered, unable to say more with the lump in my throat. I waved goodbye and walked to the check in desk – my adventure had begun and in 7 hours I would be in England, my favorite place in the whole world.

The flight was uneventful and when I landed at Heathrow I felt great. Even to this day, when I land and as I step out of the plane and feel that first rush of cool morning air, a feeling a joy sweeps over me. This trip was no different. I had done it. I had flown 3000 miles across the Atlantic all by myself and I was in England.

These were the days before the Heathrow Express train that whisks travelers from the airport to Paddington in a mere 15 minutes. Back then, the best transportation into central London was via a special double-decker red bus called the Airbus. I seem to remember there might have been different routes that went to different parts of London, but basically it took at least an hour and the bus meandered all over, stopping at designated Airbus stops near hotels. I had used the Airbus last year with Kelly and knew which route I needed and that I needed to get off at Russell Square and walk a short walk to Tavistock Square and the Tavistock Hotel.

Like most hotels, check-in time is kind of late for people arriving on most transatlantic morning flights. My plane was on the ground before 7:00am and yet my check-in at the hotel wouldn't be permitted until 11:00am. These days, hotels often have places where you can leave your luggage until check-in, but either it didn't exist then or I was not aware of it.

I decided the best solution was to stay at the airport until later where I had access to toilets, food and somewhere to sit. I wandered around and found something to eat and drink. Then I sort of half dozed on a bench. I couldn't relax enough to really sleep. I was bemused that I was surrounded by hundreds of people from India also hanging about, waiting. In fact, I wrote in my travel log that it almost felt like I had landed in the wrong country as there were more Indians than non-Indians. I later learned that I had arrived on the last day that people from India were allowed to move to England without needing a special visa. Thousands of people had flown in to meet the deadline and immigration was being strict, so many families had long waits for their guests.

I was for some reason extremely concerned that someone might steal my bag, so even though my eyes kept closing, I wouldn't allow myself to sleep in the airport. Looking back, I am sure it didn't look like my bag was stuffed with valuables. True, I had graduated to my own suitcase, unlike the first trip where I used my mother's wedding luggage from 25 years ago, but it was still a cheap bag. I was wearing sneakers too which in 1986 in London screamed "American Tourist". I just couldn't understand how all those Londoners could race down the streets and hurry through the tube stations wearing cute ballet flats, or worse, pumps with no stockings. My feet ached just looking at them.

Finally, I decided it was time to leave the airport. By now I was very tired and had been mostly awake for nearly 24 hours. I found the Air Bus with no problems and the driver shoved my suitcase into the luggage area underneath the bus and I climbed aboard with my handbag, carry-on bag and a tote bag of things I had bought in the airport such as magazines and a newspaper. The bus was crowded and I ended up in a seat two thirds back by the window. I couldn't allow myself to doze during the hour long journey. As the bus trundled first toward central London and then meandered through the city, I tried to stay alert. My fear was missing my stop. My head kept drooping as I fought off sleep but I valiantly forced myself to stay awake.

The day was dry but overcast and a bit grey. As we neared Russell Square, I perked up. My stop was close. Outside the bus, traffic was surprisingly light. People walking on the sidewalks (pavements to Brits) were walking with purpose, but compared to other parts of London, this area was not heaving with people or cars.

At last we arrived at my stop and I climbed down and the driver followed quickly to remove my luggage from underneath. Then, just as quickly, he accelerated and trundled off down Euston road. I bent down to assemble my belongings and to retrieve my map to get oriented to walk to my hotel. And then my heart stopped!

My suitcase, carry-on bag and tote bag were all accounted for, but my handbag was missing. Like a fool,

I looked up at the back end of the bus that was already at the next corner and called out "Wait! Stop!" and waved my arms in the air. No one on the pavement walking by seemed to notice this crazy American calling out to a long departed bus.

Panic washed over me as I realized that absolutely everything of value was in that handbag: passport, Travelers Checks, phone numbers, and a tiny bit of money left over from last year's trip. I tried to think. What could I do? I looked around me for help but there were few people on the street and those who were there were marching purposefully toward their destinations. Then I spied a red telephone box.

Of course, I could call the police to help me. This was totally logical. My dad was a policeman in the States, and I had a healthy respect for all that the police did to help people. I grabbed my remaining belongings and dragged my suitcase to the corner so I could cross when the light changed to reach that red beacon across the road. It seemed to take forever, but I eventually reached the phone box. I had no money to call any other way, so I dialed 999 (the emergency number for those of you not British).

A voice demanded to know what my emergency was. I explained I needed the police and was put through to a police station somewhere. Through my tears, I explained that I had accidentally forgotten my purse containing everything on the Airbus and I needed help. I expected to hear concern and urgency in the reply. In my imagination, the person at the other end of the line was already signaling to someone across the room to send a squad car to my location immediately.

Instead, I heard a weary voice say "I'm not sure we can help you."

"What! Why? I have nothing and no way to pay for anything without my purse," I wailed, panic rising.

"We don't usually handle this sort of situation."

"Please!" I shrieked, really truly panicked now. "You have to send some to help me." After a few more minutes of pleading and begging, the man finally agreed to send someone. I told him where I was and I hung up.

Standing on the corner next to the phone box with my suitcase at my heels, I sniffled and wiped my tears with the back of my hand. I'd won a minor victory. Now I just had to wait for the police to arrive and they could chase after the bus. Surely with their sirens blaring, we could navigate through the traffic and catch up to the bus. I felt the faint stirrings of hope take root.

It was certainly taking a long time for that police car to arrive I thought as I kept glancing at my watch. Finally, I caught sight of something in the distance. It was a pair of police officers, a man and a woman, strolling (yes strolling!) towards me. Not rushing, not looking like they had anyone urgently awaiting their assistance. I started walking toward them, dragging my suitcase behind me and I intercepted them at the halfway point.

Of course they didn't act like they even knew the story, so I had to retell the whole thing again wasting even more valuable time while they looked at me patiently. Finally the male officer said "I'm sorry. There is nothing we can do to help you. You should probably just follow the bus and try to catch up with it."

I looked at him in disbelief! Was he really that cold hearted and stupid? How was I supposed to catch up with a bus that now had a good twenty minute head start? I couldn't even catch another bus because I had no money. I started crying again and when I saw he wasn't going to help, I looked at the policewoman and looked pleadingly at her. She at least had the decency to look concerned but she didn't offer any alternatives.

Angry, scared and dismayed, I turned and looked in the direction the bus had taken and wailed "I can't catch a bus!" The male officer had already turned and was going to walk back the way he'd come, but the policewoman had a bit of compassion. She came closer and said "Look, the next stop for that bus is Euston and it is the end of the line. If you hurry, it might still be there and if it isn't, you can get another bus driver to try to help."

At least it was something. I was still feeling betrayed by the police. I'd been brought up being told when in trouble, you should always call the police to help you and here no one seemed to care what might happen to me alone in London with no passport, no money and no one I could call.

I turned in the direction the officer had pointed in and started walking and sniffling. At the first corner I came to, I realized this was the corner I should turn left at to get to my hotel and this set off my tears again as I realized that without money or a passport, I couldn't even check in to my hotel.

I crossed the road and continued walking toward Euston Station, still dragging my heavy suitcase behind me. The road was on my right. I had to stop every so often to rearrange my carry-on bag or switch which hand was dragging the suitcase. At the next corner as I turned to switch, a big black London taxi pulled up to the curb and the driver, man in his early thirties and prematurely balding called out to me. "Luv, if you are going to Euston, I'll give you a lift. Climb in."

A myriad of emotions trampled all over themselves in my head. I knew I couldn't take him up on his offer because I had no money, but it was such a relief not to be ignored that I started crying again as I approached his open window.

"I am going to Euston and I would love a lift but I can't. I left my purse on the Airbus so I have no money to pay you," I burbled through the tears.

"Hop on in. I was on my way to lunch and I was just offering to help you. I wasn't going to charge you," he said hopping out and opening the back passenger door and heaving my luggage into the back and helping me inside before firmly shutting the door behind me.

Back in the driver's seat, he carefully pulled out into the stream of traffic and said "We're very close to Euston. I am sure we can catch up to the bus and get your purse back. Do you remember which bus it was?"

"It was an Airbus," I offered, "but I don't know which one. I got off at Russell Square."

"Don't cry, luv," he soothed. "We'll do our best to get it back."

"But everything is in it. My passport, my money….. I can't even check into my hotel."

"Don't worry about now. Let's cross that bridge when it comes," he said as he swung a left into a bus lane at the back of Euston. A row of seven red double-decker busses were lined up in angled parking spots, engines idling. The taxi driver parked up behind the busses and pointed to the second one in the queue which had a big "Airbus" logo on the back. "Go check it out and I'll wait here for you," he instructed and I leapt from the cab and ran to the front of the bus and climbed aboard.

I looked at the driver. He didn't look familiar, but nevertheless, I ran towards the back of the bus and searched all the seats in the region where I had been sitting. Nothing. I ran back to the front and asked the driver if anyone had turned in a purse since he'd left Russell Square and he shook his head.

Racing back to the taxi, I passed on the bad news.

"Then you were probably on the bus before that one. Let's try to catch it," he suggested turning on the engine and backing up.

As he accelerated into the flow of traffic, he reached for his radio and contacted his dispatcher and explained the problem.

"Can you contact the bus on the radio and find out where the next stop is?" The dispatcher agreed, and a few moments later she radioed in that they had sent out a radio message to all the busses to be on the alert for my purse, but they wanted a description.

"It is red and has two sections with zippers," I said. The cabbie, who was called Geoff according to the cab license posted on the glass divider between the front and back seats, relayed the information to the dispatcher. She also told Geoff where the next scheduled stop was on the Airbus route, and he began working his way through the worsening lunchtime traffic to catch the bus.

One by one various busses reported back to the dispatcher that no purse was found and my heart sunk and hope started dying again.

The dispatcher radioed in again asking what size my purse was. Not good with sizes, I used my hands to show Geoff a rough approximation of its size and he slapped his forehead as he grabbed the radio to send a message. He asked the dispatcher to correct the message sent to the busses. It was a handbag not a purse that was being sought. Oops. In my panic, I had forgotten that in British English "purse" meant wallet.

All this time the bus drivers had been looking for a small red wallet rather than for a full sized handbag. I was angry with myself and hoped this slip up hadn't cost too much valuable lost time.

Meanwhile, as we got close to the next stop, we could there was no Airbus in sight. Geoff asked the dispatcher for the list of the next couple of stops and decided to try to skip one and take a short cut to hopefully be waiting at the stop when the bus arrived.

It was a valiant effort, but traffic was chock-a-block and we were not moving fast and often were sitting still in traffic. Geoff was not running his meter but it was using up his petrol and he wasn't picking up any paying customers. Plus, he'd been on his way to lunch and now an hour later he hadn't had his lunch.

He checked in with the dispatcher saying something I didn't understand and then he pulled up in a side street and parked. Turning to look through the glass partition, he explained the new plan. The busses were all on alert and if the handbag was found, it would be taken to the bus depot at the end of the drivers shift.

"So while we wait, I'm going to take you to your hotel and I will come back to get you and take you to the bus depot in a few hours when we know that the bag is there."

My face must have shown my dismay. "But I can't check in," I started to explain.

"Don't worry about that. I will go in with you and explain the situation."

I tearfully agreed to the plan and he slowly made his way back in the direction we'd come from and eventually we pulled up in front of the Tavistock Hotel. Geoff helped me out of the cab and carried my suitcase up the few steps and into the lobby. He escorted me to the check in desk and expertly explained my predicament.

To my relief, the desk clerk was understanding and agreed to check me in. He just told me to be sure to bring my passport to the desk once I had it back and handed me my room key.

One problem solved, but it all hinged on the handbag being found and that was still an unknown. Geoff and I squeezed into the elevator with my luggage and traveled to the third floor. He used the key to open the door for me and helped me settle in. I barely noticed the room or the requested view. I just felt an overwhelming wave of worry and tears leaked out of my swollen eyes.

Geoff sat on the bed next to me and put his arm around me. "Don't worry luv. It will all work out."

"But what if they don't find it? What is someone found it and kept it?" I asked.

"That won't happen, but if it does, passports can be replaced at the embassy and your Travelers Checks can also be replaced. I'll help you if that happens, but have faith. I've told the dispatcher where you are staying and your name. We just have to be patient."

He stood up and looked at his watch. "It's 12:30. I'll ring you back around 2:00 and we can check in with the bus depot. If your bag is there, I'll drive you to the depot. In the meantime I'm going to get me lunch."

I thanked him and closed the door behind him as he left.

Now what? I had no money to get lunch but I was so stressed, I wasn't the least bit hungry. I didn't feel like unpacking and I didn't feel like reading. I just wanted to cry. So I did. Big wet sobs poured out of me but dried up after about 5 minutes leaving me feeling spent but less panicked.

I checked out the bathroom and was pleased to see it was nice and had a good toilet. The room was every bit as good as I had hoped for. I looked out the window and saw my view was of the leafy Tavistock Square and was indeed a good view.

Lying down on the bed, I was torn. I felt exhausted and wanted to sleep. I'd been up over 24 hours now but I was afraid to sleep. I wanted to call my dad to let him know I had arrived and was safe, but I knew if I told him about my problem, I would start sobbing again. So I got under the covers still wearing my clothes and put on the television and tried to distract myself.

I must have dozed a bit because I was suddenly startled awake by the loud brrrrring brrrrring of the telephone.

"Hello," I answered.

"Hello Miss Phillips?" asked a brisk female voice.

"Yes, that's me," I replied.

"I'm ringing from the Bus Depot to let you know that we have your handbag. It was found by the driver and he has just turned it in to the lost and found. You can pick it up any time."

Relief flooded over me and washed the feeling of panic away as if by magic. I felt my energy level go up (of course the unplanned nap may have helped with that) and now I was antsy. I would not be entirely relieved until I had that handbag in my possession again.

Feeling better, I got up and opened my suitcase and transferred my clothes to the drawers of the dresser and the wardrobe. Turning off the TV, I also noticed that the sun had broken through the clouds and the day was now bright and sunny. I opened up my carry-on bag and retrieved my toiletries so that I could brush my hair, touch up my makeup and brush my teeth. I was starting to feel human again.

The phone trilled again and I ran from the bathroom to answer it. It the desk clerk telling me that Geoff was asking for me at the desk. I said I would be right down and I quickly grabbed my room key and headed for the elevator.

In the lobby, I ran over to Geoff and gave him the good news. He grinned and gave me a quick hug. He led the way out of the lobby doors and into the street where his cab was waiting. As I climbed into the back seat, I leaned close to the partition.

"I feel so grateful but also so guilty that you've lost out on so much business helping me today. I insist that you run the meter for this trip to the bus depot."

"Oh, that isn't necessary," he protested.

"Yes, it is. It is my way of saying thank you for all that you've done for me. You have been my knight in shining armor."

He grinned and finally agreed to start the meter going. Traffic was lighter again in the lull between lunch and rush hour, but the journey was long. The depot was in some far western suburb of London that I'd never heard of before.

During the long journey, Geoff and I chatted through the glass partition and he asked a lot about my plans for the coming weeks, where I lived in the States and he shared a bit about his life as a taxi driver.

By the time we were nearing the bus depot, the meter had been running about 45 minutes and I realized that I had a problem. All my money (in the handbag) was in Travelers Checks except for a few coins left over from last year's trip. I couldn't pay for the taxi trip with Travelers Checks and I really couldn't afford to pay for the return journey either. I was pondering my options, when we arrived and Geoff directed me to go inside while he waited.

I entered the door and found myself in a cavernous space. A few busses were parked in the far reaches but none were close to where I was standing. A sign told me that the lost and found window was straight ahead and I followed the concrete path forward.

Similar to British Post Offices, the clerk at the desk was behind glass partition with a revolving piece in the middle that could be swiveled to transfer items from one side to the other. I approached the window eagerly.

Next to the windows was a sign that said "To claim lost property, you must pay a fee equal to 10% of the value of the item." I felt a sense of dread. All my Travelers Checks were in that handbag. If I had to pay 10% of their value, not only would I not have enough money left to cover my expenses for my remaining three weeks, but how would I pay the fee with no cash?

A sour looking woman with tight salt-and-pepper colored curls and big glasses perched on her head greeted me with a not overly friendly hello and I explained who I was and why I was there.

"Oh yes," she said, turning away and rummaging somewhere below the counter. When she reappeared, there was my lovely, red handbag in her hands. I grinned.

She said "that will be 10 pence please."

I hesitated. I wasn't going to correct her on the value of that irreplaceable possession but I also didn't have the 10 pence.

"All my money is inside the bag," I said pointing through the barrier glass at the handbag.

Calmly, she opened the handbag, found my wallet and clicked open the change purse. Thankfully I did have some coins in the wallet. She extracted a 10p coin and held it up at eye level and looked at me for permission to take it.

I nodded that it was OK. She dropped the coin into her money tray, clicked the wallet closed and replaced it in the handbag. Sitting the handbag on the revolving tray, she twirled it so that it transferred the bag to my side of the glass where I eagerly snatched it before it could disappear again.

Opening the bag, I looked inside. Not a thing was missing! My passport was there. My Travelers Checks were all accounted for, my address book filled with needed phone numbers including Ernie's, and my hotel reservation papers were still neatly folded and in their proper location.

I thanked the stern woman profusely and rushed back out to the taxi feeling a sense of amazement that I had indeed managed to get my handbag back despite the odds thanks to Geoff.

From the backseat of the cab, I held up the bag for Geoff to see, grinning from ear to ear.

"It's nice to finally see you smile," he said watching me.

"I can't tell you how grateful I am that I met you, and for all you've done to save the day for me. You are fantastic. I dread to think what would have happened if you hadn't stopped and offered me a ride."

"It was nothing," he replied brushing it off, "All in a day's work."

As he turned to start the engine, I spoke up. "I hate to have to say this but I can't really afford to pay you to drive me all the way back into London. I need you to take me to a chemist so I can buy something and cash one of my Travelers Checks. That way I will have cash to pay you but then I will need you to drop me off at the nearest tube station."

He looked a bit disappointed, but agreed. He drove to a Boots Chemist and waited with the motor running while I ran in and purchased a bottle of shampoo with a large Travelers Check. I felt like a criminal for some strange reason with my get-away car idling outside, but the cashier didn't think anything of it.

Returning to the backseat of the cab, Geoff took off again and headed toward the nearest tube. As he drove he casually asked "Would you like to go out for a coffee sometime if you aren't too busy?"

I smiled. I did want to see him again and I was so happy he had asked. "My first few days are kind of filled up," I said thinking of those plans I had made to prevent my panic "but I'm here for three weeks and next week is completely free at the moment. I would love to go for a coffee," I continued even though I'd never had a cup of coffee in my life before! I thought the British only drank tea.

"OK, well I have your number at the Tavistock. I'll ring you next week," he agreed.

A few minutes later, we pulled up a tube station I had never heard of before and today I still can't remember which one it was. I gave him double the amount showing on the meter and insisted he keep it as his tip for everything he'd done to rescue me. He tried to return some of the money but I wouldn't accept it.

I got out of the taxi, said thanks and goodbye and descended down into the tube for a long train journey back to my hotel. As I sat on the train, hugging my handbag close, I ruminated on the roller coaster of emotions I'd ridden that day and what a stroke of luck it had been that Geoff had stopped to offer me a lift. I shuddered to think of what the day would have turned out like had that not happened. I also marveled at how, despite the many panicked moments during the day, I hadn't once thought about going home. Two years ago, my panic was much less justified – caused by disappointment and worry. Today, I had a legitimate reason to be panicked and I was truly panicked but I hadn't wanted to return home. Maybe I had grown up a bit in the past two years.

I returned to the hotel and did a proper check-in with my passport and then went out to get a bit of dinner. My appetite had returned along with my joy at being in London. Returning to my room, I fell into a deep and dreamless sleep.

The next morning I awoke refreshed and excited at the coming three weeks. I would be seeing Ernie for dinner that night and next week I'd see Geoff again for coffee. Before leaving the hotel to begin exploring with a spring in my step and my handbag firmly attached to my body, I quickly wrote a letter of commendation about Geoff and sent it off to his cab company as soon as I found a stamp. I wanted the world to know that good Samaritans do still exist.

The trip was a success. I did see Ernie several times, but Geoff never did call for that coffee and it remains one of the mysteries of my life to wonder why not. When I did finally fly home three weeks later, I didn't know it would be my last trip for six years, but I did know that I had slain my dragon. I had traveled alone to London and despite an unforeseen difficulty, I hadn't raced home again.

After my six year travel break so that I could move out of my parents' house and do some more growing up, I did eventually resume traveling again. Although I branched out and visited other countries, my heart has always belonged to London and I have started going back to London alone, twice a year in recent years. I still visit with Ernie and I still love exploring this city, but I have to admit, I always look closely at the face of every taxi driver I see, looking to check if it is my Geoff, my knight in a black taxi.

Reflections on my Childhood - Alan's Early Years 1952 – 1973

by Alan Richardson

Short biography: Born 1952, three months too early for parental credibility. Lived his early life in the Durham (UK) coalfields. Son of a long line of business owners ranging from mainstream construction contractors to joiner and undertakers. The family can be found in various graveyards and the local crematorium around the Durham area. They could be described as an affable lot.

There are places I remember all my life, though some have changed. Very old words from a very young band called the Beatles. So which bits will I remember? Maybe early childhood to teens, teens to married and then such a lot of grey living it seemed such a waste. Or was it? What did the later years bring? How do we measure its worth?

Could I write a book about it? I think not! It hasn't got the world-changing requirements of a life of social responsibility. Could I write some interesting facts based upon my life? Well maybe?

This is a real treat not to have to cite every statement and justify every paragraph. It is a random reflection upon my life and the events and changes that have taken place.

Where to start and why? "Maybe those that went before me, and some are dead and some are living, because in my life I loved them all." (Beatles)

Let's have a look at the early years.

I was raised in a house with an inside toilet, oh joy as most people at the didn't have inside loos. Still we had ice on the inside of windows over the winter period. The summers were long but the year had very distinct seasons, Christmas, my birthday, bird nesting, marbling, summer holidays, conkering and then Guy Fawkes night, before repeating the cycle. It is strange how you remember the early car registration numbers like the Standard 8 number, XBB360 or the Ford Consul number UYN 460. Why, oh why, do we carry this around with us?

The summer holidays were Blackpool, Butlins at Skegness. Why was the journey out longer than the journey home? It still puzzles me to this day.

Plastic sandals made patterns on your feet from the sun whilst playing outside with other children. The only way you were allowed in the house was if it was raining. There was no TV on during the day, other than reading and painting. We made our own amusement.

My father's work allowed me access to sawdust and this made a perfect bedding for the birds eggs. As far as I am aware this hobby was legal at the time. (With the exception of protected species). A full day out roaming the fields for nests was the norm between April and June. Cliffs were climbed, trees scaled, marsh land reconnoitred and hedgerows scrutinised for different varieties of eggs. When you found an egg, the only way to retrieve it was to place it in your mouth and descend. We climbed some mighty heights for a single egg. You would never take more than one egg from a nest. It was a sort of a gentlemen's code of conduct. The key was to know whether it was dipped or not. Dipped was a term for a fertilised egg that had a chick inside. We did this by seeing if the egg floated. Floating eggs were fresh and could be blown out. The art of blowing a house martins egg was very skilful indeed. It required a tiny hole in either end made with a hawthorn spike. The contents were then blown out very slowly to avoid any damage to the shell. After all that effort to get the egg, the last thing you wanted to do was break the shell.

Summer holidays started by loading the luggage into the two tone Ford Consul with white wall tyres and settling into a journey frequented by stops to give the engine a rest and let it cool down. None of which were necessary, but it gave the adults time to picnic and smoke cigarettes. The journey was always a big adventure and destination Blackpool was always taken on a country road where the car could be made airborne. I still do this to this day. Crazy I know. The game was, 'let's see who can be the first to see Blackpool tower?' The hotel was the same every year, the Claremont on a corner near the North pier. The fishing off the pier was fruitless but it passed and afternoon or two. This fishing on holiday is ingrained in me and I have fished all over the World since.

Today playing conkers is banned as a school yard pastime; because it's too dangerous!!!! We climbed cliffs and trees and yet still managed the risk ourselves, without a bloody risk assessment. Conkering was a day out to collect the conkers. Days spent soaking them in vinegar to toughen them. The scoring was great because if you beat a conker with 20 wins, your conker became a

21er. If you had a high scoring conker it was always a dilemma to bring it back into the contest as they were often damaged from previous battles. Health and safety is just a way of stopping people enjoying themselves

My greatest tree felling was a 9m high tree for which I was chastised by my parents as it was on someone else's land. However I had help from my father to get it back to my bonfire before the owner could find out about it. Fireworks were bought individually and kept in a shoe box prior to Guy Fawkes night. A three penny banger was a powerful piece of kit. I remember my father saying to me, "The atmosphere is electric tonight", prior to starting the bonfire with paraffin and newspapers.

Newspapers were at a premium because they were much smaller than today's and they were used to light coal fires every day. The best bit of the night was to stand around in the freezing cold and cooking potatoes in the embers of the bonfire. They always tasted of paraffin, were burnt in the outside and raw in the middle. That didn't stop us burning our mouths on them.

Sitting in my grand parents' house listening to the radio as the football scores came in was a wonderful experience. Granddad Ralph Elliott was a quiet man who went through the First World War with the Durham Light Infantry. He never spoke much about his time in the trenches. I have wonderful memories of his greenhouse and giving his tomatoes a drink. The sun always seemed to be shining. The smell of that greenhouse cannot be erased from my memory. Nor can the smell of the joiners shop at Dixon Elliott and Sons

Builders. Shavings were 300mm deep on the floor to keep the bench joiners feet warm and the smell of freshly cut wood was intoxicating. Their telephone number of 174 gave away the era when they were most successful. Edward Street in Durham was named after Edward Dixon Elliott who was the patron of the Builders in 1850. I remember my grandmother saying; the war years were very profitable due to building air raid shelters. This was carried out with an Italian 3 geared wagon that had to be loaded and unloaded by hand. Ironic that they made money using an Italian wagon, a German one would be even worse.

My uncle Ralph was nicknamed Ralph the sunshine boy. He was a raconteur who liked to drink beer and was very kind and loving to me. He took me on a trip to France, Switzerland and Italy when I was nine years old. It was a bus trip from Durham bus station with two drivers, Bob and Alf. The on-bus, singing was a daily ritual which comprised of, "It's a long way to Tipperary" and this rapidly transformed into "It's a long way to tickle Mary"! The bus was loaded onto the cross channel ferry where I heard the train being loaded on board from my bilge bunk. These are great memories, so great that I took my daughter back to Reims when she was nine years old to keep the experience alive.

Let's not forget my Grandmother as she treated me like little Lord Fauntleroy. My grandmother was a Dixon and grandfather an Elliott. Both Border Reivers names. The Border Reivers were a wild crew, prone to excess. Drink featured heavily in their lives. Cooking sherry was an ingredient of all meals. I never realised it wasn't a serious part of cookery until I was in my twenties. When Emperor Hadrian conquered Britain he stopped at our relatives, as were we too wild and pagan in nature for the educated and urbane Romans. I take claim for the building of Hadrian's wall in Northumberland due to the need to keep my unruly relatives out of England.

It is strange to think that we never spent equal times at each of our grandparents. Grandmother Richardson never featured highly on the visiting list. I remember calling to see her one afternoon after a matinee performance at the Majestic cinema and she cried openly. We visited slightly more after that. I wonder if it was because my father had built a house for his mother after work in 18 months and all she gave him was an overcoat. He met my mother at the same time and managed a bit of courting in between. I'm thankful for that as I wouldn't be writing this otherwise. With my predicted arrival, he set to and built another house in his spare time. There were fatter prisoners of war than my father by the time he had finished building two houses. I would say he nearly worked himself into an early grave.

So when success came, with a timber building company, Taylormade; he enjoyed the spoils of victory and led the high life with good dinner jackets, cigars and guess what, lots of drink. Mother had a wardrobe full of cocktail dresses and shoes for the lavish parties thrown in the dance hall by the pool.

The parties went into the early hours and often ended up in the swimming pool or the turkish bath room. A retrospective fly on the wall may have raised an eyebrow at the behaviour. I often wondered what went on? Maybe it's just as well I don't know, but I have my clues. After all this was the time of the Profumo scandal and people were making up for the austerity of the war years.

Where did I learn to swim? Self taught, no swimming club or lessons for me. In a private pool where I could set the lights to suit my fancy. My parents and work colleagues would drink cocktails at mid day whilst I was swimming. They were very excessive days! I had the pool to myself 99% of the time. It was a massive blow when I went to the public baths and they wouldn't clear it out so that I could have my usual swim. I didn't understand.

By the time I was ten years old, money was no object and the manifestation of this pinnacle of success and excess, was the building of a new family home, Beechcroft. Beechcroft was a house made famous for the party scene in the cult movie, "Get Carter". Due to the building of this house, I had my first encounter with a woodsman's axe to fell 30m high beech trees, thus clearing the site and my first encounter with concrete. If only I had known how much concrete would play a part in my life I would have treated it with a little more reverence. I do remember how heavy it was; too heavy for a 10 year old boy.

The building of Beechcroft gave me a wonderful playground and I still remember at 10 years old, smoking my first cigarette in the rafters when it was being built. No health and safety in those days. Girls were just coming onto my radar in the nicest possible way.

At 11 years old came the 11 plus examination. This was my first taste of failure. I was always in the top 5 at school and twenty passed the eleven plus. I'll never know what went on that day? However I do remember it well. The examination was at the boys' grammar school. We had to take the bus and walk a mile to get there. We had coffee at an Italian coffee shop on the way back to school. Eleven years old and left to our own devices to travel and find the school for our exam. No chaperones were considered necessary. No wonder young people are taking longer to grow up!

At 11 my voice began to break and St Mary Magdalene church encountered the mystery screecher. Charlie Baxter was the choir master and a very good organist. My behaviour declined with the breaking of my voice and Charlie decided we should part company. Church twice on Sunday and choir practice on a Thursday night no longer had the attraction it once held. An old school friend, Ian Duncan and myself decided upon a leaving present, of putting the choirmasters bike up a tree, letting his tyres down and throwing away the bicycle pump - we thought this was an appropriate leaving present. Boy did we get into trouble. Stuart Knox stepped out in front of a car and was sent flying after evensong. He only received a broken arm but what an impact it was. Kids are no different today, it's just that they are immobile and sat in front of a screen of one type or another unable to look after themselves.

Eleven years old had me building a tree house at Beechcroft. Building and flying model aeroplanes in the garden that was about an acre in area. The reading of model aeroplane plans and assembly was up to me at 11 years old, no help was offered or asked for. My expertise with an aluminium framed catapult destroyed part of the woodland bird population. I could hit a bird at 40 metres with unerring accuracy. A very cruel pastime not just for me but for my friends who took part. The autumn migration when the birds roost around the tree house was carnage. Nothing to be proud of there!!! I did make friends with a tawny owl that took to roosting in my tree house. At dusk the owl would arrive and land on my wrist to be fed strips of raw bacon. I wore my mother's leather gloves to help prevent the penetrating claws from going into my wrist. Once or twice the claws hit the bit between my glove and green anorak. A photograph shows me and my tawny owl and the lid of the old radiogram in the lounge that had a polished sprung hardwood floor for dancing.

Alan and tawny owl – Beechcroft 1962

The radiogram was sought because it had push buttons to select operating functions. This was the same as a juke box in Blackpool. According to an old mate

(Lawrie) it had massive bass speakers and you could listen into the police wave band. More of this when I arrive at Belle Vue Terrace, after two house moves from Beechcroft!!!

Our family comprised of 8 or 9 pairs of uncles and aunties on both sides of the family, however on my mother's side of the family they were great aunties and uncles. Bricklayers, business owners; Spitfire and jet test pilots.

The number of relatives that visited Beechcroft once we moved in was legendary. There was a constant stream of visitors. Strangely I became very popular with my peers and I had a wonderful relationship with Peter Turnbull, a police officer's son who read DC comics with me in a kind of silent companionship. We sat in our conservatory for hours reading.

Chopping down beech trees provided the greatest opportunity to build the biggest bonfire ever. So big we had a camp in the middle of it. The smell of fresh cut green timber was intoxicating; it was so strong you could taste it. One Saturday morning we felled a beech tree onto the bonfire to save moving the branches and a group of teenagers came running out in terror as they had camped out overnight in my camp. They should have been terrified as the branches penetrated the ground to a depth of 2m. God help them if they had been impaled.

I remember my headmaster asked for a composition of our journey to school. To go to school, I went through the fence to school so it was a short composition. My memories of school were towel bags and hand washing prior to lunch and the headmaster telling those at the back of the queue to go to the front because those that are last will be first, after all it was a CE of school. Good bible grounding to go with Sunday school and St Mary Magdalene choir. Singing and church played a huge part in my life as it did with all of the Richardson family before me. All buried either at the church or Belmont grave yard. We collected sunny smiles stickers for foreign babies and children and also had a card for key liturgical milestones identified with lovely stickers. You had to attend church or Sunday school to receive a sticker. I wish I had kept them.

Leaving Belmont C of E school for Gilesgate Secondary Modern was a hell of a shock. It also meant a substantial change of friends as most of my friends went to the grammar school. There was a late starter to our year called Mike Frost. He was to become a very reliable friend. Our gang consisted of me Mike, Lawrie, Jim, Youngy, Keith and Colin. We went to the cinema on Friday nights and skated at most other times. Pupils were streamed according to their ability. How times have changed. There were recognised losers and everyone wasn't equal. A little more honest than the system we have today. There were to be more groups of friends before I was 21.

Skating took up a lot of my free time. After walking two miles to the ice rink, and skating for two hours, we would clean the ice with hand pushed scrapers for a free pass. Then a 2 mile walk home or maybe the bus if cash permitted. There was a group of 7 friends that skated regularly. We had our own corner for changing. It was very territorial. These were very happy years and we were very much like pack animals in behaviour. We all customised our skates. I dyed my red and black kangaroo skin boots to all black to look meaner. You just know I went faster in them!!!

The lengths we went to sharpen our ice skate blades were excessive, we would anneal the blades in the metalwork shop at school, create razor sharp u shaped edges with Ward files, then case harden them after they were sharpened. Our hockey boots cut the surface of the ice into pieces. We were super fit and our legs were strong without any defect. I wish I could say the same now. However they have given me good service.

I had the good fortune to have "Brains" as a friend. He could rebuild radio sets from Russian tanks used by ham radio operators. That got him into trouble with the Post Office for transmitting illegally. These were pre citizen band radio days. Rubber duck hasn't been born yet, nor had ten four. The air was full of offshore commercial radio stations. Caroline north and south were the big players but many coastal towns had their own broadcasting ships. Fishing in Eyemouth was a joy listening to radio Berwick.

The problem was; how to get a decent reception. No problem. We had "Brains". He took a wireless up into my sister's bedroom and ran a 300 ft wire washing line from the third floor to the end of the garden linked to the old hot valve set. This was the equivalent of assault, on the old brown radio with Bakelite knobs and an illuminated panel with long, medium and short wave bands interspersed with the radio stations worldwide such as Istanbul, Reykjavik, etc. why is Reykjavik embedded in my mind. This was before the 'Cod War' days. The Cold War was still high on the agenda.

Once a decent connection was made, a whole new world opened up. Depending upon the atmospheric conditions, radio waves bounded around the atmosphere and were received by our washing line. The French had the Maginot line. We had the washing line. Ours was much more fun and intriguing.

The old radiogram was much more interesting. It had FM and this meant we could listen to police broadcasts. Brains had built a testing device called a grid dip oscillator, (Grid - controlling mesh element inside a thermionic valve, Dip - drop in valve grid current due to external resonant circuit absorbing RF energy from instrument's RF Coil, Oscillator - generator of kinetic & audio/radio etc. electromagnetic energy - Grid Dip Oscillator).

This fiendish device blocked radio signals to determined parameters only known to Brains. Well did we block police Communications? Of course not! This thing was designed to have a very limited range and therefore such nonsense was impossible. Or was it? Obviously a flight of fancy on my part.!!! We were a mischievous lot and coupled with intellect that made us cleverly mischievous. This is much worse than thick as a brick mischievous!!! As an observation and being prone to collect bits of paper called qualifications, they do not change your intellect. You just gain a wider knowledge. We were inquisitively bright and looking for something all the time. Who the hell needed the Internet.

Do you know? My grandson said the other day. "Granddad you must be very knowledgeable". I said no, I just read a lot. Reading about other people's lives, whether it be new scientific ideas, personal relationships and pastimes, it all makes your mind broader, and better for the author sharing their experiences. Maybe this sums up this smorgasbord of life?

1966 was the year of the World Cup final, held in the UK. Sunderland won the FA Cup in 1973. My mother polished our coal fire poker holders, made from brass shell cases to within an inch of their lives, watching these matches. We all sat around our black and white television in what is now my sister's front room. Parents and three friends, Mike Frost was always there as he and my Dad got on famously. This was to repeat itself later with friends yet to be discovered.

The World Cup came and went in 1966. However, prior to the actual World Cup matches we watched Russia and Italy train at Maiden Castle on the banks of the river Wear. Kicking balls back to the world famous Russian goal keeper, Lev Yashin was a big thrill. We miskicked three brand new World Cup footballs into the thicket and then pretended to look for them. The journey home with a football each was very exciting. Theft did not come easily.

My first motorbike was a James 197. A Villiers engine and no clutch cable. We rode it around the bridle ways that surrounded our village and over the old scrambles track at Belmont. I had fallen off my push bike there so many times between 7 and 11, riding a motor bike without a crash helmet wasn't so bad. I still have the scars to record those falls. We put a quarter of a pint of oil in to see us through and evenings' entertainment. It was gone after an hour. I shared the bike with Arthur. He and I also used to go fishing at Roker in the Wear estuary. 1966 was quite a year.

My first band seen live, was at Carrville Working Men's club near Durham. I remember a cover of the Stones' 'Satisfaction' that was amazing; no alcohol there or for some time. Some bands were very good. I progressed into Durham City and saw groups at Alington House and Dunelm house. Arlington house was defined by purple strip lights that made white glow in the dark. It was where I met my first wife. She arrived in a bridesmaids dress after the marriage of her sister. Local bands cut their teeth in this environment. Dunelm house was a brutalist concrete structure of the 60s and had some amazing bands playing. A night out comprised of 4 beers for 10 shillings, 5 shillings into the venue, totalling a 15 shilling night out. Great music and pissed to boot. I often had cornflakes when I got home and was sick in my waste paper bin. A little too often for comfort!!!

My interest in music had us driving to Bath on June/ 28/1969 to attend the Bath Rhythm and Blues festival . We set off on Friday afternoon to arrive early Saturday morning.

Some Other People's Lives

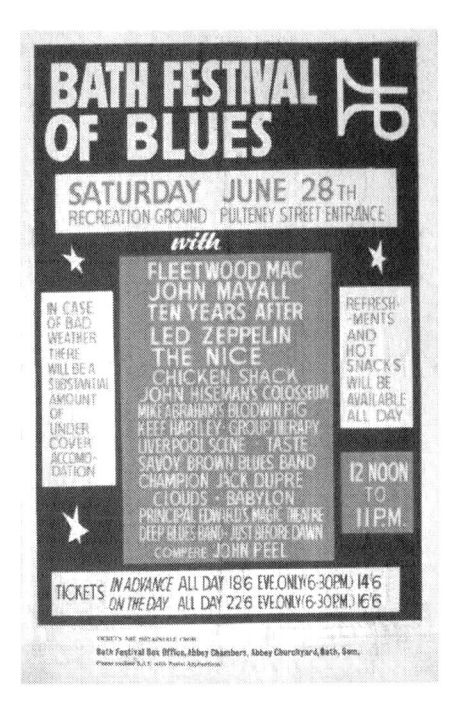

Advertising poster (http://www.ukrockfestivals.com/the-69 Bath-Festival.html)

Our party comprised of me, Joe Egg, alias Alan Hay but he took a lot of acid, hence the Joe Egg. Jeff Morland also alias Barking Billy and the Rhythm Dogs. Geoff O Brien was the car owner. Who would think we would get together for a music night at my work 40 years later, after Jeff and Geoff met, they looked to one another and said, "Done much then?" I had my flabber gasted – 40 years and that was it? Back to the road trip to Bath. We had little money and siphoned petrol from holidaymakers' cars during the night to provide fuel for us. The car that belonged to Geoff O Brian was an Austin Seven. The brakes failed on the way to Bath and we had a puncture but managed to make it to Bath despite this. A high risk transport strategy. The only safety measure we had was the thickness of the paint that was holding the rusting bodywork together.

The headline groups were: Fleetwood Mac, 10 Years After, Led Zeppelin, John Mayall's Bluesbreakers and Chicken Shack, whose pianist left to join Fleetwood Mac shortly afterwards. All of this for under two pounds Sterling. Why were the days so warm and sunny?

We didn't eat all weekend. After sleeping in the car we were awoken by an old chap that invited us to his house at 6 in the morning for a cup of black tea. Another beautiful sunny day. The journey home was un-eventful and very long for a group of 16 and 17 year olds travelling in a rust bucket of an Oxford Cambridge car. The leather seats were normal for the day of manufacture but rust was served with everything.

The first scooter (Vespa 150). The scooter was an ex-police machine. Petrol had lead in it and caused carbon deposits that required decoking. Rubbing the head down using plate glass and emery paper increased the compression ratio but made starting a bugger; a little knowledge is a dangerous thing.

I bought my first car off David Evans, a vicar at Durham cathedral. I still visit the garage that housed the car. We sealed the deal off for one soft top Sunbeam Alpine for £150 with a sherry. He was a lovely fella who said his parishioners couldn't get in and out of the car due to the low seats.

I loved that car and was forever balancing the carburettors and flushing out the old oil that got very dirty in those days. The points and condenser were always ready to be replaced and you wouldn't undertake a long journey without a spare set. The arrival of my car announced the departure of my scooter. How things have changed.

Alan and car – green shield stamps and Cleveland fuel (all long gone) 1969.

Following finishing my exams at school I attended Durham Technical college.

Durham tech was where I met Geoff O'Brien and a load of sharp lads were on this course. Their intellect was awesome. Everything we did was from first principles. Maths was our daily bread. We worked from 9 to 5 every day, except Friday when we finished at 3.30 with General Studies. These years have put me in good stead for a work ethic.

My next educational establishment was Charles Trevelyan Technical college. I started one week late as did Ken Smith from Tynemouth. We were instant friends until his life ended at the age of 49. I was one year younger. His birthday was 09.03.1951 and we hung out with Mick Robson who also had a birthday of 09.03.52. These became two very great friends. Not to last very long, due to cancer, bugger. As Jimmy Mc used to say – "Life is a lottery!!!!"

I'm sitting here writing this with retirement looming in a couple of years. These friends were my investment in the future, companionship for my retirement. With age I've found golf is one of the few pastimes I can manage, we could have been golfing partners? What could have been? That is the question? Well I can be definite about the answer to this. Gone is gone and they only live in my mind. Thank the Lord I have the memories.

When Friday night comes around and I fancy a beer and some company, the available list is much less due to the grim reapers relentless efficiency. So when I ask for whom the bell tolls. It isn't my time just yet. It has been a twisting and turning life of varied experiences and I've never been one to pass up a new experience when it availed itself. Choirboy to passing Buddhist, carnivore to vegan and back again. The love of two wheeled transport and fishing has never left me, it just rose, fell and rose again as the tide always does. As an old mate Geoff O' Brien once said. "I looked all over the World for happiness". When he stopped looking it was there all of the time. Maybe that is true of most of us?

Marriage came in a quiet way. My father wasn't coming to the church until the last minute because it was a Catholic Church. However after one of many heart attacks he relented his anti catholic views following a visit from a priest. As he said, when you think you're knocking at the gates of heaven any comfort is very welcome. Needless to say that one didn't kill him, hence the tale. One of the best events in my life was the birth of my daughter, but that is too personal for this piece.

Following the birth of my daughter, we had regular trips to Pudsey (Leeds) to visit the brother and sister-in-law, weekends consisting of Friday night to Sunday at Fartown (Far Town or Fart own, it's all in the pronunciation). Fridays nights were composed of drinking and playing darts on a Yorkshire board, made of a tree trunk soaked in water and without a treble ring. Saturday was spent with the kids playing and having days out. Sunday lunchtime was half a gallon at least, then gingerly driving home on Sunday evening after a sleep. One night my brother-in-law and I had about 8 pints of hand pulled Tetley's beer in two hours and we were busting for a piss going home. I stopped the car on a long straight road. Barry jumped over a wall for a piss and I thought, that's too much of a leap so I tried going over the wall 20 feet further uphill. A very poor decision.!!! I jumped over and fell 12 feet through the air. Landing knee deep in mud and cow shit. That will teach me not to drink and drive. However everyone did in those days, hence busy pubs in the middle of nowhere. They were happy days that continued for many years. I'm lucky to have these as memories.

The telephone call at my in-laws one Friday night is never good when it is 11.30; you just know it can't be good news. I'd been out with my brother and father-in-law for a drink and upon my return I was told to return to my old family home. The old man had asked me to look after the family when this happened as he said, "Those bloody junior doctors don't know what they are doing, they will kill me". That was about 3 months before his death and now there he was dead in the chair, his prophesy fulfilled. The organisation of the funeral was up to me at 21 years old. I had the weekend to organise the funeral and a team of men to sort out on Monday morning at work. There was very little time for self pity. My mother was lost without him and hit the bottle very hard. On the day of the funeral a writ was being served due to lack of cash flow in the business. Uncle Archie sent the bailiff away and this bought us a little time to think of a strategy for survival. There were going to be some very difficult times ahead to sort this out.

What do I do?

Further education to complete; or save the family business? Take care of those around me? I did make a promise to my father to look after my mother, so it was try and get a failing business back on its feet. This was the start of the business years and the end of my childhood and youth.

On reflection it worked out reasonably well with a little help from – my friends, yes, but more importantly from above. Beatles more famous than God?, Now there's a thought.

Some Other People's Lives

In the MDs seat at 21 years old

The Diplo Cricket Match
by Geoff O'Brien

This story, as the title suggests, is about a cricket match. But first I will give you, the reader, a little background. I graduated as an engineer and then spent two years in London working as a Civil Servant. Part of my job was to read relevant journals and the financial press. Whilst I really enjoyed my job I did not feel that this was my destiny. One day I came across an ad which asked the following questions. Do you have a degree in electronics? Do you want to travel and earn a tax-free salary? That ticked all my boxes. In a matter of weeks I resigned (my mother was mortified - giving up suited steady employment with a pension for a lad from a mining community - well you can work it out!) and became a doodlebugger!

What is a doodlebugger I hear you ask? Very simply doodlebuggers are part of the oil and gas exploration industry - they are insects that wander about in circles. We do the initial surveys - if things look good then a drill crew takes over and see if oil and gas is present! What did you actually do as a doodlebugger? Very simply, we sent a lot of energy into the ground. This then either reflects from different rock strata or refracts and travels further into the earth and can be reflected back by deeper strata. We recorded the reflections using very sensitive microphones and the time it takes to travel back to the microphones gives a measure of depth. Essentially we mapped strata looking for areas where oil and gas could have accumulated.

How did you send the energy into the ground? Again it is not rocket science. You can drop a big weight, use dynamite (my preference - I loved dynamite!) or use a vibrator. Vibrator you say. Yes but a bloody big one (as a quick aside when I lived in the USA my colleague and friend, Bruce, a Kiwi, had a job title of Vibrator Engineer - he loved giving out his business cards - he always received interesting responses from women. My job title was Field Engineer - no competition!).

Anyway let's get to the story. At the time I was based in the Sindh province in Pakistan. We lived in camps. The expatriates lived in trailers and the local crew lived in tents – this was known as the base camp. In total we had about twelve expats and about 300 locals. It was an organised, almost militaristic sort of environment. Each day we would travel to our work sites and from time to time we would move the base camp when travel times became too long. It was a very mobile operation.

I had just returned from leave and was informed that we would be moving to a new location. But instead of moving the base camp we would be establishing a fly-camp. A fly camp is a temporary tent camp. The tracks to the new area were so bad it would have been really hard to move the base camp. Normally fly camps consist of tents but fortunately we were told they had found a suitable place to set up camp, a house and compound apparently belonging to former governor of the area. An advance crew left a few days before we were due to move to set up the kitchen, portable generators, buckets for the shower and charpoys. These are wooden frames that are strung with light rope and used as a bed.

On the day we moved to Diplo we finished field work early and we were driven (we used local drivers) to the fly-camp. We entered the compound, and in front of us were a group of young men playing cricket. When they saw us they grabbed their gear and fled.

Our new home was a two storey structure with a large veranda overlooking the compound. It was a bit of a rambling structure but looked as though it would be comfortable. I asked the cook about the boys playing cricket.

"Ah Sahib they seem to play most days of the week." Yes there was still a touch of colonialism!

"Why did they run away?"

"I think, Shahib, they thought you would be angry with them for using the compound"

"Really - what time is dinner?"

In about two hours I was told. After a short discussion we decided that we should take a walk around the village - sort of introduce ourselves. We insisted that our labour leader, Rafiq Mohammed, join us. He was highly respected by all and spoke fluent English. Off we set.

Diplo was an interesting place. It seemed a little like it was a bit of faded glory. There were no paved footpaths or roads but many of the buildings were well built. The primary material was dried mud brick. As we walked Rafiq was approached by a group of villagers.

"Is there a problem?" I asked

"No! These men have brought a message from the village Headman – he wants to meet you and show you around his village. "

This was an invitation we could not refuse. Keeping good relations was very important to our operations. We met and after much shaking of hands we started our tour. We were steered to see the village's prized asset - the generator. We were taken to a building, the doors were flung open and there before us was a diesel driven electrical generator. We were told that this was operated for two hours a day in the early evening. Luckily we had our own generators back at our fly camp!

As we walked around the village I saw quite a few young men. Many of them approached and introduced themselves. Most of them spoke good English. I asked the village headman, through Rafiq, why the level of spoken English in the village was high.

"Yes" said the Headman "We are very proud of our schools here. Many of our children go on to university."

I asked if any of the young men who were following our village visit could be the cricket players. If so, could he tell them that they were welcome to play cricket in the compound at any time. We would park our vehicles elsewhere.

Next day we returned from the field and sat on the veranda watching the cricket. There were two Brits, two Aussies and one Kiwi who struggled to explain to our

American colleague the rules of cricket. The next night we were invited by the boys to join the game. "Why not!" I said, and so we did. I was great fun! However, the state of their equipment was very poor. We decided to ask the office in Karachi to send some cricket gear. We felt that this would consolidate a good relationship with Diplo. That was radioed in and we went back to our routine. Life in the field is very routine.

In about four to five days two large cardboard boxes arrived. We placed them on the veranda. The boys were playing. We waved them over and started to open the boxes. We were all stunned. The boxes contained two full sets of really good cricket equipment. Bats, bowls, stumps, bails, pads, gloves and caps.

"Come on let's set them up" I shouted. We did and had a really good game. After the game we told them to take the cricket gear to their homes. They were very reluctant to do so and after some discussion it was agreed to keep it at the villa.

We then asked Rafiq to speak to the village Headman to explain that the cricket gear was meant as a gift to the village. A few days later the boys asked for a meeting. They expressed their gratitude for the cricket equipment and asked that we celebrate by having a proper match – Diplo boys versus the oil explorers! This would be tricky as normally we spent all day in the field and that would leave little time for a match. However, we agreed to finish early. We agreed a day for the match and asked the boys to invite people from the village to come and watch the game. We knew that we could adjust our logs so that it appeared that we were working as usual.

On the agreed day we stopped work early and headed back to Diplo. As we drove through the village it appeared to be deserted. As we approached the compound I could see that the veranda was fully populated with the Headman and his entourage. A large blackboard, no doubt commandeered from the local school, was set up as a scoreboard. The wall around the compound was fully populated by the villagers. It was clear that that the game had attracted a lot of attention.

We completed the formalities and won the toss. We elected to bat first. The wicket, if you could call it that, was hard. I received the first ball. When the ball hit the ground there was little bounce and it rocketed close to the ground. Fortunately it missed the wicket. I managed to hit the next ball and we were off. We did manage to score a few runs but the wickets began to fall much to the delight of the crowd. Our American colleague really mesmerised everyone by holding the bat is if it were a baseball bat. He did manage to hit a few big ones before being caught on the boundary.

I began the bowling and I was unable to get the ball to rocket along the ground. What I did manage to do was to get just enough bounce that presented the ball to the batsmen at the perfect height for it to be thrashed to the boundary. Most of my over was. The crowd cheered every run scored by the Diplo boys. They quickly passed our score and the game was over. There was much cheering and polite applause from the veranda. In the spirit of cricket we all shook hands, waved to the crowd and left the pitch and went to the veranda to congratulate the Headman on the skill of his team.

We continued to play cricket. We left Diplo about ten days later. We did a formal handover ceremony of the cricket equipment before we left. It was very touching. I wonder if anyone else remembers that match, or if any of the boys went on to become professional cricketers? I don't know but the Diplo cricket match remains very fresh in my mind.

Fly Fishing Idaho
North Fork CDA and the St. Joseph River
by Tony McCleary, USA

Chapter I

    I need to set the stage a little for you. It all started when my work took me to Idaho, Jan 2012. Knowing this would be a good opportunity to learn about local trout streams, I scoped out the local fly shops. Northwest Outfitters, an Orvis shop, were more than accommodating. I actually had a beer with a couple of the guides and bought some flies in trade for information. I made up my mind that if given the chance, I would make it back there to fish. Coeur d'Alene, Idaho is an absolutely gorgeous place. Mountains surround, with Coeur d'Alene and Hayden lakes tucked in between. I found there to be several options for trout fishing, the Coeur d'Alene River (CDA), St. Joseph (St. Joe) and Kelly Creek to name just a few.

Many months passed after that trip and another opportunity did indeed rise, to head back to Idaho for work. This time it was in mid-September and my gear went with me. I landed in Spokane, WA, on Sunday afternoon, got my rental car and the adventure started.

I pulled up to my first fly shop, Silver Bow, in Spokane Valley, WA. Two drift boats sit in the parking lot and a Golden Retriever greeted me at the door. This is my kind of place and I'm sure to find something good in here. I was offered a lot of useful information; local flies that were producing fish, rivers to focus on, ongoing hatches and time of day to hit the water. He mentioned using a two fly combo. I have used that in the past but not in the combinations he suggested. I was used to a hopper/dropper combo. He talked about two nymphs or two streamers. The flies he sold me were great and of course had to get an additional trinket or two. Yes, it is an addiction.

After a short drive I got to my hotel, in Hayden, ID, got settled in and headed to my next fly shop. Northwest Outfitters was a definite stop, as I had been there in Jan. Pat and Brian were again very helpful, as to what flies were working, local hatches and river access locations. Northwest Outfitters is in an upscale strip mall setting, stone front to the build and impressive look. They had a great selection of flies, fly rods and gear.

Both fly shops mentioned the CDA, North Fork CDA and St. Joseph rivers. Another river brought up was Kelly Creek. But, it was a little too far for the time I had to invest. The Kelly originates in the Bitterroot

Mountains, in Montana. I hope to fish this on my next trip.

As I was driving from the airport, visiting the fly shops, I noticed a smoky haze. Apparently, a lot of Eastern Washington was on fire. The smell of smoke is very prominent. The news reports that several hundred thousand acres of forest are a blaze.

It was off to work on Monday and Tuesday. The training was going good and my students were doing well. But, all I could think about was hitting the local trout water. A few of my students had their own ideas as to where to fish, as they also fly fished. Lucky for me, their thoughts coincided with both Northwest Outfitters and Silver Bow. The decision was made to go after work on Wednesday.

Wednesday was a good day of class but I couldn't wait to venture around the wilderness. I chose to go to the North Fork CDA. It was only 45 minutes away and should leave enough time to fish 3 hours. I followed the CDA, along I95 until I came to Kingston and then headed north. I went about 2 ½ to 3 miles and found my first put in. My companions included me, myself and the good Lord. He is always fishing with me.

I got my waders on, rod strung and bag ready, I was off to the races. Trout were rising in several spots. I studied the river a bit and decided to start with an Adams dry, my go to fly. The water was crystal clear with some current but not a lot. I cast the Adams a few times and decided that wasn't working. I switched to a PMD and started to get some interest but no fish in hand.

I couldn't seem to land anything. I was in about 3' of water and just out of reach of another set of rising fish.

I decided to relocate a bit into the river. The first step was good, the second step was good. I have been fly-fishing and wading streams all over the country for 20 years; it didn't seem too difficult. The water was now just above my waist. I took my bag off my waist and threw it over my shoulder. The third step was an entirely different story. I took that last step and put my right foot on what I thought was level rocky bottom. It turns out the water was so clear I misread how deep the water was from that point. My foot slipped off of that rock and I now have a bit of water coming in over my waders. The cold sensation was getting down to my feet. I tried to step back but the current was just enough that I couldn't retreat. So, I decided to take yet another step forward, hoping it would get shallower. Again, I miss interpreted the depth of that particular stretch of water. To my surprise the water was deeper. At this point, I am bouncing off the bottom trying to stay above the surface. All in all, the depth was about 6" over my wader top. I took one more step and decided to tread water and swim out of the situation. I looked and felt like such a buffoon. In all my years, I have stumbled in streams before but have never had water come in over the top of my waders.

Through all of this, beginning with the third step, all I could think of was I had my cell phone and a camera. I had one on my hip and the other in my waders. What an idiot!!! Why on earth I needed a cell phone was beyond me. I quickly swam out of the situation but not before I was completely soaked. My waders were about half full when I got out. Yes, I looked around very quickly to see if anyone had witnessed this misadventure. I got my waders off, took my cell phone and camera apart and laid everything on the rocks to dry. Nothing left to do but continue fishing and hopefully dry off some. I fished for another 45 minutes and said the heck with this. I gathered my wet gear; put my wading boots back on and tried to find a shallow area to cross.

The biggest disappointment is all I had to do was head north about 100 yards and I was in water no more than a foot deep. A lot of lessons learned on this outing, so far. Don't get greedy, slow down, look for a better place to cross. It goes without saying; this was not my greatest outing. I got very wet and caught no fish. The scenery was phenomenal but not enough to make up for the misfortune. I drove back to the hotel to get my wet clothes off and relive what just happened.

I went to work the next day and couldn't help but tell my story. My cell phone didn't work and I had to put it in a bag of rice to hopefully dry out. My personal phone survived, remarkably.

Chapter II

It is Friday now and I am over my last outing, ready for a new adventure. I didn't have a lot of time so I headed back to the North Fork CDA. This time I went further up the mountain on Little North Fork Road. I parked at an old unused campground. The weather was great, about 62 degrees, slightly overcast. The smell of smoke and haze is still in the air. I was in the shade of the mountain the entire evening. The water looked perfect; the temp was great and ready for rising trout. I made a few casts without any action. I again started with an Adams; quickly changing to a Purple Adams, from Silver Bow. That was a key change. The cutthroats responded very well. The first catch/release was by a deeper riffle along a log jam. Fish were rising and they couldn't resist the temptation. It was a very heavy 15" cutthroat. She had beautiful color and a wide girth, a heavy fish for the length she was. That made Wednesday night all but a distant memory. I kept fishing towards a bend in the river but time was getting away from me. It was getting dark and I was quite a ways from the rental car, but I had to keep fishing as long as I could see.

The interest in the Purple Adams died off a bit so I switched to a BWO. This was one that I brought from Minnesota. A half hour passed and several casts were made with no luck. I decided to go back to the Purple Adams, which had landed me one fish already. I had a fish rising off to my right and the first cast was a bit short. Second cast was right on the money but missed the rise. This looked like a decent sized fish and kept my interest going. Finally, I made the needed cast upstream and he took it. What a strong fish!! The West Slope Cutthroats don't disappoint when it comes to fight. They are a heavier, stronger fighting fish compared to the Browns and Rainbows of the Midwest. This was indeed a good fish pushing near 18". I landed the fish and quickly released it. Did I mention that my camera was also in my waders when I took that unplanned swim on Wednesday?

I took no pictures of these two catches. It turns out, these two fish were some of the bigger fish of the trip.

It is now dark, two fish released and it feels like a monumental achievement, comparing to Wednesday's mishap. I headed back to the car and had to take a different route. I headed back through the willow brush instead of following the stream. In talking with Brian, Northwest Outfitters, I asked if I would run into any critters along the way, moose, mountain lion, elk, bear, etc... Brian said I could run into any of the above but to be most cautious about the moose. About halfway back to the car, I ran across some moose tracks, not too fresh but at least I knew there was at least one in the area. I never ran face to face with the moose and made it back to the car without incident. Can't say that I was too concerned and I generally carry a large fixed blade knife just in case. I usually carry the knife in case I get caught up in a river and need to cut something free, but it would work as self-defense also. Although, not sure what that knife would do to the moose, I would most likely be trampled before I unsheathed it.

Chapter III

I woke up early Saturday morning, with the intent to be on the St. Joseph River by 9:30. The sun was just rising over Hayden Lake with a cooler breeze out of the Northwest. The waking up part worked but it took longer to get there than anticipated. I followed the instructions from Northwest Outfitters and took Moon Pass, south out of Wallace. It is a road that unless you know where it is, you will never find it. I stopped a man on the street to ask, he responded, "Are you taking that car on Moon Pass, it is all gravel road?" I responded with, "It's a rental." He thought that was perfect and chuckled. He was kind enough to tell me where the road was and I was off. As I entered Moon Pass, it did indeed turn to gravel. I noticed several signs along the first mile or so. One sign said, "Gravel – One Lane Rd, 33 miles." Another sign said, "Single Lane road, with turnouts". I grew up on gravel roads but did feel sorry for the rental. The scenery was indescribable. The sun was shining with a slight yellow hue. As you look off of this single lane road, the trees were enormous. As I ventured up and over the mountain, I was looking down on those same trees. My speed never exceeded 30mph due to the switchbacks, gravel and of course the scenery. I found many places that I could do a drawing of. The trip on this gravel road took me through 7 tunnels, all of which you didn't want to meet anyone on. If you met another vehicle, one was going to have to back up to let the other pass.

Picture says it all

View while on Moon Pass, South of Wallace, Idaho

    I finally arrived in Avery, ID, exactly where they told me to. I stopped at a gas station to get a little more information and something to drink. I got the drink but little information was offered. I decided to head up the mountain about 5 miles. I put in at a long sweeping curve, next to a log jam. I noticed a lot of fly fisherman out and thought it was as good a spot as any. There were no fish rising, none!! I went ahead and tied on a BWO, dry flies are my absolute favorite to fish. I got the rest of my gear on and proceeded to work my way down to the water. This wasn't exactly an easy venture but I made it without incident. Or, so I thought. I made several casts with the dry fly, with no interest. Tying on a nymph and indicator for the next round, I noticed that I had lost my net. Damn it, just what I needed. After several casts and yet another combination, I headed back up to the car and to find my net. Luckily the grass wasn't too tall. I broke down my rod and loaded everything up to relocate.

This is the site of my first put in on the St. Joseph, 2 miles upriver from Avery, ID.

I went up stream about 2 miles to a little slower water that had several bends. Not having luck with dries, I tied on a nymph. This time I used a #12, bead head pheasant tail and a Caddis as an indicator. I had a couple of takes but no fish. With nothing on dries or nymphs, I tied on two streamers, an Irish Fennimore and a Mickey Finn. I continued to have no takes, catches or releases. After about an hour and a half, I called it quits and headed back to Avery to get a bite to eat, pondering the entire trip back to town, "What am I doing wrong?" If there were fish in this river they didn't want anything I had!!

I pulled into the Trading Post, the local watering hole. It was like stepping back in time, at least 40 years. Everyone turned their heads when I entered. They quickly went back to their conversations but had to see who was coming in. There were about 30 people in this joint. Most of them were locals with one big group of 4 wheelers. I sat at the bar and ordered a Coors. It tasted so good, after my disappointing day, so far. The bartender looked like he had been there at least 40 years. The beer was cold and the menu looked good. I ordered a cheeseburger and another beer. It was one of the best meals of the trip, partly because I was so hungry. The bar was such a homey place, decorated in old nostalgic items, like crosscut saws, fly rods and beer posters. There was even a skeleton in the southeast corner. Evidently, a body found out in the forest, probably a frustrated fly fisherman. My thirst and hunger have been quenched; it is time to get back at it.

After pulling out of the Trading Post, I noticed a fly shop on the river side of the highway. Yes, I stopped; it is an addiction with me. The owner had a few suggestions and a couple more flies to try. If you haven't been keeping track, I have acquired quite a selection of Idaho flies. He had a great shop, full of flies, fly rods and the normal gear. At the back of the shop, his kids sold ice cream. I would have partaken of some but I was still full from the cheeseburger. As I checked out, there was a cedar strip canoe hanging above the door. It was gorgeous and for sale. My wife would have been proud; I didn't buy it but would have loved to take a cruise in it.

Chapter IV

It is about 3:30 and I am 9 miles upriver from Avery, continuing to try and locate trout. The sun is shining bright with a few wispy clouds floating around. The smoky haze is still present but not as much. There are fly fisherman everywhere I would like to stop. I finally see a 200 yard stretch of very slow water and no one is fishing it. There is a bend up ahead of me and a lot of exposed rocks. Behind me is a log jam that the water is being diverted around to the left. I get my gear on and go back to a dry fly, a Purple Adams. I toss out the idea of a two fly rig and go back to what I know best, a single dry. I am seeing fish rise, Halleluiah! I am back in the game. Three casts into this and I have a cutthroat on, a nice 12 incher. Make sure my fly is good and I am back to casting. I slowly work my way upstream along a narrow feeding lane to the left side of the river. It is about 3' deep with a bit of rock and log structure. I decide to switch to a PMD and there is another one on, this day is taking on a pleasant twist. I quickly release the 10 incher and stay with the PMD.

I headed another 2 miles upstream to a rope and wood plank suspended walk bridge. This is one of the most gorgeous places I have ever fished. The setting was out of a movie or the best fly fishing dream I could have ever created. My gear is still rigged with a PMD and it worked before, so I don't change a thing. The river is again below the road edge. I work my way down to the water and lose my glasses. Oddly enough, this is the second time today I have lost them. Once again, I retrace my steps and find them. So far, my net is still with me, but the evening is young.

14" West Slope Cutthroat, caught on St. Joseph River

Hot spot, where my first St. Joe cutthroat was caught

Up ahead I see two fishermen working towards me. Behind me I have 3 entering the water, along with a yellow lab. I am starting to feel pressured but stick to my ground. I cast to another rising fish under an overhanging limb. He takes it but I can't land him. I cast back to the same spot and this one is mine. It is another nice one, about 14". All told I took 7 fish from this pool. Earlier, I was worried I may not find fish in this river. Feeling the pressure of the others crowding me, I decide to pick up and move.

View of Rope Bridge, another trout hotspot

This spot, just upstream of the bridge, is quite a bit deeper. Deep slow moving pools on the road side and shallower fast running riffles to the mountain side. I sat a bit trying to figure out the plan of attack. It wasn't long before I saw a few fish rising alongside an enormous boulder, with the riffle running ahead of and beside.

I cast my 9' rod with its 5 weight line to the first rise in the riffle. No takers and the fish keep rising. After a few more casts, I switch to an Orange Caddis. Fish on!!! This one isn't big but it is satisfying none the less. Now I have lost my glasses again, in the river, just beneath me. Good retrieve on the glasses and I am back at it. At this time, there are about 8 fish rising within a 20 yard stretch of this faster running riffle. A lot of smaller fish and I am trying to selectively find the bigger ones.

I move downstream toward the boulder and a little slower deeper water towards the tail end of the riffle. These fish seem a bit bigger. They are making small slurps, taking spinners off of the top water. I again change flies, going to a Griffiths Gnat and they are responding to every cast. I missed the first two that took it. Third time is the charm, fish on. This is a nicer fish, must be 14", another heavy fish like Friday evening. Grab the net, landed and took a picture. Yep, my phone is back in business. The camera still hasn't come back to life.

Staying in the same spot I can see a nice fish rising to my right, up behind the bolder in a small pool just off of the riffle. This one will be tricky keeping my line mended long enough for the fly to stay a few seconds, without a drag. Five casts to this fish and he is tightening the line. It is a good day. No fish for 4 hours and the last 2 hours have been steady. Evening fishing has to be the best for this river, this particular trip. It is a nice 16" cutthroat, not as heavy as the one before but still a nice fish. I must say, I am impressed with the quality of fish on the St. Joe.

The fly shops had all talked about a trout that I wasn't familiar with, a Bull Trout. I had never heard of them. They stressed how important it was to release them without bringing them out of the water. Apparently they are reintroducing the fish back to the area or protecting what remain. They are a very large fish and I was in hopes of one taking my fly. To my disappointment, it was not to be.

Moving on to a stretch just under the swing bridge, the water slows and gets much shallower. The trick is taking the bridge out of play and keeping my line away from it. This was a good spot with two more fish released. It is getting dark and I had best make my way back up to the car. Shouldn't be hard, I didn't get more than 100 yards away. I get my gear off and put away, then decide to check out this walk bridge. It is rather dark out now, but feel the need to walk across. Even in the dark this bridge is quite cool. I shine my flash light down into the water and could see several trout stacked up and still feeding. What a sight!!

This day ended with a total of 12 cutthroats and all of them caught in the last 5 hours of the day. It took me 3 hours to get there via Moon Pass, so I opted to travel back on the highway to St. Maries. It seemed like a good idea but holy buckets this is one long and winding road. It is at least all blacktop but I can't seem to raise my speed above 50 before the next turn or stop sign. I finally get to St. Maries and turn north. The Moon is out bright and every river crossing seems to reflect its rays. Nearing Coeur d'Alene Lake, I start to see a lot of lake front homes, with their lights shining across the water. It is about 10:30 and the traffic is light, so my trip home is faster than the trip down to Avery.

I spent the day fishing with no cell phone coverage and it was awesome. Or so I thought. Due to the mountains, there are many areas with little if any cell coverage. Unbeknownst to me, my wife had been trying to reach me all day. Fearing the worst, that a Mountain Lion had attacked and eaten me, she was quite upset when I called in. I was very surprised the National Guard hadn't been called in to rescue a fisherman having the time of his life. One of the greatest things about fly fishing is the solitude and a cell phone generally disrupts that. One exception is the sending of text with a photo of the latest catch to a buddy that couldn't make the trip.

It was quite a day, one that I won't soon forget. Struggling so much early in the day to finally figuring out what they were wanting. The scenery, fishing, solitude, weather, beer and cheeseburger were all phenomenal.

Chapter V

It is Sunday morning and wake up rather tired from the day before. I decide to do some laundry before I head out fishing. This is the last day of my 6 day license, so I know I am fishing today. Yes, I do know that laundry should never come before fishing but I knew I would be getting back late. I headed back to the North Fork CDA but decide to go much deeper into the mountains. I ran out of paved road and once again on gravel. I must have been 15 miles in on Little North Fork Rd before I stopped. I found a small remote campsite on the river side or South side of the road. I back in and get ready. It is quite a hike down this steep slope but all is well. I still have my knife, flashlight, compass and am ready for a long evening of fly fishing.

I decide to start with a PMD, I caught 6 smaller cutthroat under 10". I switch to another dry and very little response. Brian, Northwest Outfitters, told me to try an Orange Caddis dry. I had 4 of them in my box and thought this was as good a time as any or better yet my last chance to try them. I am seeing only a few Caddis in the air and fewer on the water's surface. The first cast provoked a rise, so I knew this was going to be a good one. I cast again, this time a little upstream of the last cast and the water exploded. This trout wasn't going to let this big bug go. Grab the net and he is landed. I took a good picture and quickly released. One down and hopefully many to come. I continue to fish this pool, catching two more.

North Fork CDA

I decide to move upstream a bit. This water is extremely shallow with fast running riffles feeding two pools about 2' deep. Trout are rising all over the feeding lane going into this first pool. Still using the Orange Caddis, I make my first cast to the back end of the riffle.

My line gets tight and I quickly raise my rod. It is another smallish cutthroat. I caught two more fish in that feeding lane and noticed what appeared to be a larger fish towards the head of the riffle. I move forward a bit to get a better angle but casting to this fish is made difficult by the riffle and the low hanging branch. First cast came up short. Second cast, hits the tree. Third cast appears to be perfect but no rise. Fourth cast, again, is right there but nothing. I know he is just sitting there being picky. I am determined so I throw a fifth cast and bang, he is on. He tries to take me into a small log jam and I fight him backing up into the stream. I let him tire himself a bit, strip him in, grab the net and he is landed. He may be the biggest so far at 18". Nice fish. Not as heavy as the one on Friday night, but a nice fish.

I release him and keep going, headed upstream. A bend in the river is up ahead about 300 yards. I am hoping to get there before calling it a day. As I am working my way, the fish get a bit more closed mouthed on me. I caught a couple smaller cutthroats on a smaller dun pattern but nothing spectacular. It is getting dark now and get the feeling I should start heading to the car. All told, I caught 11 fish today, another great day harassing trout with a fly rod. Just can't beat it, good fishing, great scenery and awesome weather.

I decided to step out of the water and head back on land. It was one of the weirdest feelings walking on this hollow sounding ground. This area had so many down falls, root beds that have silted in over the years, it truly sounded hollow as I walked through. The canopy above was so tight very little light shone in. I had the flashlight out just to get through the trees and by now it is completely dark outside. My waders are wet, gear is dirty and everything needs a bath. My rental car especially needs a good bath.

Monday Evening, I stopped back by the Northwest Outfitters to say, "See ya" and to thank Pat and Brian. We had a good laugh over my swimming escapade. They are a good bunch of guys. I, of course, I had another beer with the boys. I believe it was Trout Slayer this time, made by Deschutes Brewery. A very good choice I might add, considering the trout I was seeking.

Overall, this trip was one of the very best for trout fishing. The training I was instructing was good. The people of Idaho are special people. Leaving Idaho and headed to Utah. I hope they have trout there….

The End…..until I fly fish again.

Austrian Interlude
a memory of a day on the road to Greece in the summer of 1969

by D Telfer

Heat shimmered off the road reflecting upwards and making their eyes smart. The traffic was more scarce now and as the numbers dwindled further so did hope of ever getting away. That morning, the place seemed an ideal spot to hitch a lift but now, after eight hours of standing forlorn in the roadside dust and litter, it just felt like hell.

They were somewhere outside Graz, en route to Greece. The trip had been planned during what had once seemed interminable Sunday afternoons at school. An older brother had hitched to Greece via Istanbul with a friend the previous year so it seemed obvious that they should follow. They had pored over the map of Europe trying to picture places that had been described to them but were now just names and discussed possible routes as if they were old hands. Should they take the overland route and travel behind the Iron Curtain through Yugoslavia and Bulgaria or drop south into Italy and take the ferry from Brindisi? The northern route had prevailed and here they were in Austria.

The heat and dust made time drag heavily. Boredom and thirst in equal measure drove them to visit a small roadside stop from time to time to buy a cheap soda. Money was strictly rationed as each had set out with a meagre £30 which had to last six weeks so Cokes and Pepsis were replaced by local brands in a vain attempt to economise. Their sickly flavours and garish colours did little to satisfy either need but at least it was an excuse to leave the glare of the roadside and enjoy the relative cool of the halt. Locals stared at them at first but as the day went on the stares turned to glances and eventually they began to be ignored altogether.

As the afternoon dragged on the heat intensified and the two sagged on the dusty verge now not even bothering to turn and look after cars as they passed down the road into the shimmering haze, all hope gone.

At last the temperature started to drop and light to fade. The two went into the rest stop for a drink and because there didn't seem anything else to do. They sat dejectedly in a morose and exhausted silence, staring into space. Their reveries were broken by the entry of another into the room. He was tall with blond hair knotted into a ponytail and a straggly unkempt beard. His clothes were brightly coloured and loose fitting and he wore open toed leather sandals. He was quite the dirtiest individual either had ever seen before with road dust matting everything and nails so black they appeared to have been painted. Seeing the two, he approached and spoke.

"Hi". His voice was well modulated, but that was the only thing that was clear as his next words were in German. When it became obvious that no-one had a spoken language in common, guesswork and signs took over. It was obvious that he too was hitchhiking and was on the hippy trail and they both caught the magic word 'Katmandu', although whether he was going to or from there was not clear. He bought sodas and the mood became more positive and nods and gestures became more animated.

By now the light had faded to darkness, and beyond the lights of the rest house it was pitch black away from the roadside. The German stood up and indicated he was off to sleep. He gestured to the two to follow, and picking up their meagre baggage, they followed him. He set off purposefully across the road and it seemed he knew exactly where he was going. Suddenly he turned away from the road and plunged into the woods that fringed it along a narrow path. The two faltered and came to a stop. They exchanged glances and there was an unspoken anxiety. Where was he leading them? Was he really alone? What to do? As they stood, more aware of the wood by sound and smell rather than sight, the German turned back to them and impatiently gestured to them to follow. Sticking close together, the two followed him, senses straining and adrenaline beginning to flow.

The path was narrow and twisted between the trees with only the lighter hue of the sky silhouetting their tops giving any sense of direction. They were conscious of a slight descent, and in the distance they could hear the sound of running water. The descent continued and the sound of water grew stronger. Suddenly they were out of the trees and into the open, the path giving way to a more uneven and rocky surface. It was still pitch dark with no moon and light cloud obscuring any faint starlight. They could just make each other out and the two saw that as far as the German was concerned, this was journey's end. He produced some sort of blanket from his bag, lay on the ground, covered himself and turned to sleep. The two followed his example and lay down too but at a little distance from him and huddled close together. The sound of the water and the exhaustion of the day both conspired to overcome their fears, and soon they both slept.

Brilliant sunlight was their alarm clock and both awoke within moments of each other. Of the German, there was no sign. They both looked around amazed at the scene that greeted them. The sound of the water came from a fast flowing river, flecked with white and silver but of the most brilliant blue, coursing rapidly through rocks and gullies.

Shortly below the beach, for such it was, it met with another larger river with water of a duller hue from the tiny pieces of sediment carried with it from the mountains from whence it came. Both flowed through heavily forested valleys and high above them they saw a schloss perched amongst the trees like a child's toy gleaming white in the morning sun. The whole scene was so perfect it had the air of a photograph selected for a jigsaw puzzle rather than reality. Neither spoke as they took in their surroundings. They picked their way over the larger boulders that fringed the smaller river and drank the crystal water and bathed in a freezing pool. The heat and dust of the day before all washed away, they turned to follow the path back to the road; they were renewed.

And a Rod for the Cat
by Lawrence Milner

The end of a holiday had never bothered me much. Wherever we stayed, no matter how nice the places, they had no great hold on me. Whilst packing for our return journey we might comment, "Maybe the weather's better back home.." or "It'll be nice to get back to our own beds." And so we would return to beautiful Durham, sufficiently consoled. However, this was not to be, many years ago, when our last week-long fishing holiday came to an end.

We had rented the same cottage with its fishing beat on the Teviot four years previously, during May, when the trout fishing was good but the wind was cold and very discomforting. That year, 1984, my father, my brother, his friend, Sid, and I spent the week fishing, freezing, and looking after Sid. Sid was what appeared to be a pretty helpless character who, we found, could not cook, wash up, or make his bed. As part of our housework team, he was nothing short of quite useless. He was also insensitive to our hints, which became less subtle as the week progressed. Justice was innocently done, however, on a number of occasions.

For example, I recall the time when I persuaded him to throw a good size grayling back into the river because, I judged with my then ignorance of this particular species, that it wasn't edible! As he reluctantly placed his catch back into the water and watched it swim to freedom, I informed him, as I thumbed through an angling booklet I always carried at that time, that the grayling was apparently considered a delicacy "similar in taste to the salmon". It was to be his only catch that week! Then there was my father, who could not restrain himself from pillaging Sid's funds, having discovered his lack of talent with a pack of cards. There was some deep and searching digs into Sid's pockets around the late night card table.

Despite Sid's one and only attribute, which was his amazing ability to make my father quite rich in the short space of one week, he did not get an invite to our next holiday. He had, I have been informed, recently married. I hope his wife was more successful than we three in trying to domesticate him. I believe my brother and his wife later holidayed with Sid and his 'better half'. Now that's what I call friendship.

But for this trip the line up was to be quite different, and consisted of my father, myself, my darling Jacqueline, the two children, Simon and Joanne, Kim the dog and Ming the Siamese cat. Quite a car full.

My father was a real fishing fanatic. He once admitted to me that he would rather be angling on a river than be drinking with his friends at the local, and he loved his pint "amongst the company", as he put it. He was not, I would say, a particularly 'clever' angler, but what he may have lacked in experience and reliable knowledge, he more than made up for in an unfloundering determination to catch fish. And catch fish he did!

Myself, well I like to think myself a more scientific angler than my father, but our catches were invariably similar. Perhaps because we so very often fished together.

Jacqueline is a wide-eyed, country-loving woman, who fished with a 'junior angling kit'. I suspect she derived greater pleasure from observing the wildlife around the riverbanks than she did from actually fishing.

Simon, at thirteen, was still in his restless youthful phase, where he couldn't seem to stick at anything for any length of time if there's nothing doing to keep his interest (like a battalion of soldiers attacking a position on the opposite bank, for example). Consequently, he did not catch an awful lot of fish, one exception being our 1985 holiday, fishing the river Orchy prior to the start of the summer salmon runs. He caught numerous good size trout in a stretch of river a little way upstream from the Dalmally bridge. He was fishing with a worm on ledger tackle and just couldn't go wrong. There must have been a waiting list to get on his hook that day.

Joanne, a little girl of eleven, stuck with us whatever we did, and would try anything without having to take it too seriously. Joanne had a 'junior angling kit' too. She was set to be a teenager soon, and we would lose her to the boys and the discos of teenage life.

Kim was a lovely Sheltie bitch, much loved, very faithful, and extremely lively at thirteen years old. She wanted to be with us wherever we went, and so she was a constant and sometimes irritating companion on the riverbanks. She tolerated Ming, who would often ambush her and swipe her across the nose. Now Ming was an amazingly playful Siamese 'kitten' of six years old. I was never a cat lover, but then I'd never known a cat like Ming. Such character, such playfulness, such interest in people and such facial expressions I had never before seen in a cat. Dog loving friends would listen sceptically as I tried to explain how I, a dog lover for fifteen years, became so attached to a cat. Of Ming, Joanne would say, "He's the only Ming in the world", and, of course, he was.

There was a 'no Sunday fishing' rule imposed on the river, and so it was decided that we would leave Durham mid Sunday morning and spend most of the day completing the mere seventy mile journey at a leisurely pace. We would stop for a picnic and exercise our animal companions somewhere along the way. As was the usual practice when travelling to a fishing destination, my father and I cast a keen eye over the landscape as it rolled past, our purpose to observe any stretches of river or still water and postulate the presence of game fish therein. This, we found, admirably passed the time, and allowed us, in our imaginations, to fish waters we would probably never visit.

We picnicked on a site in the Redesdale forest. What a beautiful day it was. It felt like the first day of spring, with people eating their packed lunches and walking their dogs. Ming was a bit of a novelty, being the only cat present, and him being on a leash. One small dog, a bouncy black and white terrier, showed great interest in him. Ming, however, did not return the attention, as he was preoccupied with contemplating an ambush on some chaffinches, which defiantly fluttered about close by in search of easy pickings from the visitors' luncheons. The terrier pranced around us in ever decreasing circles, excitedly wagging its tail and seemingly intent upon a feline-canine meeting. Then, within yards of a confrontation, he would suddenly withdraw, disappear, and then return a few minutes later for a further circulatory attempt at a meeting. He made three such abortive attempts in all, before returning, we guessed, to the house behind a nearby thicket. A resident, perhaps, with little experience of cats. Having eaten, stretched our legs and inspected the stream for any sign of trout (of which we saw none), we resumed our journey, arriving in Jedburgh mid afternoon, too early to collect the cottage keys, which, as if an age old tradition, were unavailable until four PM.

There was a lovely public walk in Jedburgh alongside the Jedwater river, which I would have recommended with one word of warning; unless you are physically fit and used to exercise, do not, as I did, try your hand at the 'keep fit' equipment which some enterprising persons had provided along the length of this walk. These were mainly made of rustic wood, and were numbered and provided with instructions for use. However, they neglected to erect a sign saying, "Do not attempt all exercises with gusto unless you are fit". We came in on a high number, at the wrong end, and worked through them all. Now I hadn't done any violent exercise for some months, and if I had remembered the aches and pains of my introduction to playing squash after months at a leisurely pace of life, I wouldn't have been so keen on this session. And so it was to be that I would not be able to sleep for the next twenty-four hours, and, of much more poignancy, a day's fishing would be missed.

Having arrived at the cottage, unpacked, and lit the log fire, I went on an inspection walk along the river, accompanied by Simon and Joanne. It is a beautiful area. The grey stone cottage, unavailable now to visiting anglers, was visible from most of the fishing beat. Standing alone, its lawned gardens stretched some thirty yards down to the path of an old railway line. There was once a station a short distance downstream, near the road bridge, but like so many disused railway stations, it had been converted into a residence. Standing there, on the course of the old line, it was easy to imagine a steam engine chugging along on its journey from Berwick, through Coldstream, Kelso, and then down to Jedburgh. The old bridge that carried the line over the Teviot has now long gone. Whether it was brutally demolished along with the line, or whether it fell down due to age and neglect I do not know, but its remains can be seen in the form of huge grey pillars, standing alone, without purpose, on the riverbanks.

Only a few dead Giant Hogweed stalks stood upright on the once river swept banks, and, as we walked downstream, we flattened them to the ground. These things are incredibly large, being some eight feet tall with girths of twelve inches, and although harmless in their dead state, the bristles on the stalks of growing plants are very irritating to the skin, and contact should be avoided. We found a further two items which caused us some excitement, lying just above the water line. These were the bones of two sea trout or salmon, some two feet long, picked clean by birds and animals, possibly Otters or more likely Mink. With thoughts of hooking a fish as large as these, I found myself smiling in contemplation of the week ahead as we walked back along the river to the cottage, where we convened for dinner.

As I have said, there was a 'no Sunday fishing' rule on the river, and so before leaving home I had declared my intention to commence fishing at one minute past midnight, Monday morning, come snow, hail or rain, and rain it did. Hopeful of a break in the downpour, we all, except my father and Ming, that is, marched off into the darkness to a spot a few hundred yards upstream from the cottage. The rain poured down upon us, but it wasn't pungent city rain, smelling of tarmac. It was clean, warm, sweet, country rain, and I'm sure the birds and animals loved it, for never before had we experienced sounds the likes of which we heard that night. On the opposite bank of the beat upstream of ours was a small pond, and, although we could not say with any certainty, it seemed as if the incredible midnight chorus was emanating from this distant site. It went on incessantly, and can only be described as every frog, bird, duck, goose and swan call I have ever heard, all continuously sounding together. It was as if they had all converged there, in the pouring rain, to have a good shout about their travels and adventures; not listening to each other, just talking at each other. We didn't stay long fishing that night. The rain continued, and back to the cottage we went, without a fish, but enchanted by the midnight chorus. Two torches guided us through the darkness and the rain.

I have never believed in or wanted to rely on 'drugs' to cure an ailment. I'm one of those people who, perhaps foolishly, believe in a sort of vague self-curing ability. However, I was never so thankful for a couple of soluble aspirin tablets as I was that Monday. My aching muscles and aching head, courtesy of the previous day's exercise, prevented me from sleeping, which made me feel even worse, until those little white tablets broke the hold. I slept soundly for three hours and was ready for more fishing by the evening.

Teatime saw us all sitting around the crackling log fire, reading the catch record for the season so far. We knew we were too late for the main spring salmon run, but we consoled ourselves with the thought of hooking some brown trout and, well, possibly a sea trout or a salmon. One entry in the record mentioned a large bream supposedly caught and returned to the pool at the bottom of the garden. We frowned in disbelief, as did Bill, the ghillie, who had joined us for a cup of tea. Ming sniffed him at a distance and then returned to the more important business of scouting out the remainder of the cottage, taking special interest, as cats do, in the warm linen cupboards and the little nooks and crannies. Kim showed little interest in these pursuits and was happy to sprawl cosily in front of the fire and dream, whereas Ming was to be found later that evening belly-up in a washbasin of warm soapy water, held down by three adults wearing claw resistant gloves as he tried to resist Joanne's attempts to give him a much needed wash. His 'interests' had extended to the log and coal store, into which he had sauntered and apparently decided that a good roll on the coal-dust covered floor was a great idea. We might have blow-dried his fur had we been able to catch him as he raced out of the bathroom like the favourite in the 2:30 race at Ascot.

Monday evening's outing passed with only a partial turnout on the river and nothing noteworthy in terms of filling the larder with fish. Tuesday saw us all, except Joanne, fishing, for some of the time anyway. Simon lost the end piece of his rod as he made a cast. Consequently, we spent some time dredging the pool which, we guessed, being fairly slow, would not carry the piece downstream, but it was not to be found. A bad start indeed. My father provided a rod for the rest of the week. Returning upstream to my spot, I continued to fish a floating fly down a narrow deep run, where I'd seen some very good but infrequent rises to hatching flies. This stretch ran along the opposite bank, and I was to spend a good deal of my time there. Kim had other ideas. Being a Sheltie of sheep-dog stock, she had an annoying habit of barking at us if we weren't all rounded up in the same spot, and when we were fishing, we tended not to be. It seemed to upset her if we were apart, and she would express her concern by incessantly barking until, when we'd had enough, she was told sharply to shut up. This I did, and whilst turning to face her, intending to add impact to the shout, I missed a very good rise to my fly. Gritting my teeth and counting to ten, I continued to fish. Then, as I looked about me, it didn't seem to matter. The sun shone, the air was fresh and warm, and we were out in the countryside fishing a fresh, clear river. What more could we want? This beautiful serenity was rippled only by the flight of swans and duck, following the path of the river, and by the sound of lapwings, displaying their aerobatic skills above their nests in the fields opposite.

It seemed that around the same time each day, at about midday, there was a profuse hatch of flies on the river, and for some twenty minutes, the fast central stream which ran down into the next pool thirty yards downstream was boiling with fish. I only caught a couple of trout from these hatches, as I tended to approach too closely from upstream, and it was difficult to fish this stretch from below due to a large spreading bush on the bank-side.

Just prior to one of these hatches, my father, fishing a ledgered worm in the still pool at the bottom of the garden, caught the bream whose existence we had all soundly doubted. Having returned the fish to the water, the event was entered into the catch record. Maybe next week's residents would believe it. Neglecting to bring his fly fishing tackle with him when he returned to the river, he could not take advantage of the hatch. Continuing to fish on the opposite bank, from where many fish were taken throughout the season, he again fished with a worm, on tackle too light for my liking, and landed a beautiful three pound trout.

The week progressed, and Joanne, using her junior angling kit, fished happily with Simon and Jacqueline. It all looked like a family outing on the riverside, with flasks and packed lunches. I'm sure Jacqueline lost a good fish on one occasion. I had tied a prawn on the hook for her and she was letting it slowly sink, drifting down the pool, when, she explained, the line went taut and the rod shook. By the time I got there to investigate the excited calls, the cause of the excitement had subsided into disappointment and the line was slack.

We did not fish every day. Sometimes we would just walk along the riverbanks. On one occasion we walked downstream to the lower extent of the beat to see what fishing delights we were missing. Ming followed us, and met his first horse, nose to nose. The horse, one of many which followed us, playfully trotting up and down the riverbanks, had spotted Ming in the short grass, and on being approached, Ming flattened himself to a one inch piece of fur! We rescued him on this occasion, but on our return past this spot, the same horse trotted inquisitively toward us, and I lifted Ming up to introduce them. They sniffed each other, nose to nose, the horse with his ears twitching and Ming with his ears pinned back flat against his head. What were they thinking, I wonder?

Each night, before we sleepily climbed the stairs to bed, pleasantly tired by the country air, we would all sit around the fire, drinking hot chocolate and telling each other of our riverside experiences. Some of us would declare our intentions of an early rise, at the crack of dawn, and then sleep well into the morning. It was not unusual to get out of bed and find oneself alone in the cottage, staring out of the window onto the riverbanks where the rest of the party were fishing.

I fished most of the nights into the darkness, sustained by hot soup and sometimes complete hot meals in aluminium foil. The first night I stayed out late a search party was organised, comprising of Simon and my father, as I was expected to return much earlier. A quick signal across the river with my torch let them know I was safe, and I was back to my fishing. There was, I know, some big fish in the pools, very occasionally rising to fly, and although they eluded me night after night, I thoroughly enjoyed the time I spent there. The near black darkness, only experienced in the countryside, with its silence gently broken by the sound of flowing water, rising fish, and the riverside wildlife. It seemed to me that being part of this is the way we were meant to be, indulging in this serenity and earthy beauty that we tend to lose sight of, having precipitated into the hustle and bustle of our luxurious, high technology existence, largely detached from the very earth and nature that supports it.

Jacqueline said that I did not utter a word all day, the Sunday we came back home. I don't think she meant that literally, but admittedly, I was quite upset at having to leave the cottage and the river. There would be another year, though, and there was still the rest of the season to fish the river Wear around Durham. And this we did.

We returned to the cottage the following year without Kim, who sadly died not long after our return home. My father died recently, but not before I was able to take him back to fish that beat on a day ticket, fifteen years after our last visit. The memories flooded back as we both recounted those wonderful family fishing holidays. Simon and I are little wiser and more practiced on the piscatorial front, Jacqueline and Joanne more than a little more beautiful, and as for Ming, well, he has also left us and gone to the great scratch pole in the sky. Had he still been with us, I'd like to think that, coal-dust-rolling aside, he would have made an inquisitive, observant and successful angler, and that, to complete the angling family, I would surely have had to consider procuring a junior angling kit for him.

Train Spotting

by Alan Elliott

The author - to quote Peter Cook, "I was an only twin". This was a serious disadvantage to lose a sibling before life had started. However this did not stop him spending days on wet and windy railway platforms awaiting the next train to arrive. He had a khaki anorak but friends came less easily. He always had his train spotting books for company and wore sound heavy duty brogues to keep feet dry and warm no matter what the weather threw at him. The brogues have stayed for life.

As a child I spent the hot English summer days beating out railway cutting fires started by the steam trains as they passed. I would arrive home smelling of smoke and blackened by the burnt undergrowth. It's strange; November the fifth would see me chopping down trees to make a bonfire. Well I only did it once. My life was on the line after I asked my Dad to help me drag it home. He actually did do this to rid the World of the evidence. Back to the story line; in November we make fires and the rest of the summer put them out. Logic was never a strong point of mine. I was more ruled by fun mixed with a little danger.

The best challenge was to walk along the exposed edge of a railway bridge whilst a steam train passed underneath. Bloody lethal activity, yet I'm still here to write this for you. It was a 60 foot drop onto the railway lines or train, if you lost your footing. Playing chicken was about as crackers. Sitting on a railway line for as long as possible whilst a train was approaching.

We always left a penny for the train to run over and cherished the misshapen coins of the realm.

Trains have always been a love affair. There is nothing like hanging out of a passenger carriage window on the inside of a curve; you get covered in ash and smoke. Simple boyish pleasures that have never left me.

Between 10 and 14 years of age saw me hanging around the end of railway station platforms, drinking instant coffee with evaporated milk and eating cold bacon sandwiches smothered in tomato sauce. I still have my Ian Allen train spotting books to this day. Two editions, edition one was steam trains and the other edition was confined to such as Deltics, diesels, shunters, electric, diesel electric, multiples etc.

For the uninitiated. When you spotted a train you carefully underlined the number in your book until such times as you spotted all of the trains in your area. I'm sure men have inbuilt autism. Then there were opportunities for rail travel to spot more. More of that later.

The highlight of my train spotting career was when the signalling system was electrified. Manual red and white and yellow and black signals were replaced with lights. This is where I will introduce you to Uncle Bob. Uncle Bob was really my great uncle on Grandma Elliott's side of the family.

Bob was a ticket inspector at Durham railway station. He offered me and an old mate, Colin Smith, a signal each. I had that signal nailed to an exposed roof truss in my dormer windowed bedroom for most of my teenage years. My bedroom was my den.

Bob, realising I had a passion for trains, asked a train driver if I could drive a train and park it up off the East Coast mainline. Try that one these days. I would expect to see someone prosecuted 50 years after the event as seems to be the case in current times. I would prefer they were not prosecuted, but the present day righteous seem to need to persecute, or is it prosecute the elderly and judge them by current day values and not the value of the day. So foot on the dead man's pedal and slowly turned the handle to get things moving. One ring of the bell followed by a two bell reply had us halt on the viaduct over looking Durham cathedral. We then went onto another line, back through the station. Repeat the bell sequence and reversed it into a line to park it up. Nothing to it. It was only a small passenger multiple train of three carriages. I remember having to let the glow plug heat up before we fired the train up. Fifty years on and it is still as clear as the bell I heard on the footplate. Wonderful memories. I was very privileged.

I was bought a Regular Sprinty B 35mm camera for my thirteenth birthday and this super tool was what I thought to be the 'bees knees'. No more Kodak box brownies for me. I had f -stops, shutter speeds and focal lengths to consider. This was the perfect accompaniment to a day out train spotting. The more complicated it was, the more I loved it.

My best value train journey was a £5 day return to London to see a super group of their day, Blind Faith. We boarded the train at 12.15am on the Saturday morning, following a decent quantity of Guinness at the Station hotel. We - being my mates Pete and Paddy.

We were Cream fans, another super group of their time and a free concert in Hyde Park, London, was just too good miss. The journey to London was uneventful albeit it was a very long time before we arrived at Kings Cross station. We took the tube to Hyde Park and this was quite an adventure for 16/17 year old teenagers. The journey across Hyde Park was memorable as the early morning sun was strong and the sky a clear blue. The stage for the day's events was being erected and Hells Angels patrolled the park with motorbike and sidecars. The German military helmets gave them a menacing air. This was my first unescorted adventure and a certain circumspection was evident. What to do now? It was 6am and things didn't kick off until early afternoon. We went shopping in Oxford Street and bought John Mayall's latest single 'Suspicions', a misogynistic ditty with plenty of good sax. No sex, just sax. I then had my first pint of Directors bitter which was flat and awful but we all agreed it was excellent. Man's beer, but we were kids. The strawberries and cream after the beer were much better. Oh well, let's go back to the empty Hyde Park we had just left. Oh bugger, a sea of freeloading people. It was a disappointment but we heard our heroes, Eric Clapton and Ginger Baker. What to do now?

Blind Faith (http://www.geetarz.org/reviews/clapton/bf-hyde-park-free-concert.htm, accessed 11.03.15)

Paddy had gone AWOL. Pete and I went for a Chinese meal on Oxford Street. I had chicken and pineapple with boiled rice. It was delicious. It was seven o'clock and we still hadn't found Paddy. Strolling along Oxford Street we came across a low life cinema that was showing 'Joy of Sex'. This documentary about sex and masturbation was delivered by naked actors with beards; the female actors had beards at the other end. The commentary was by white coated men who appeared to be medical doctors. They probably bought their qualifications in Thailand, as people do to this day. We bought two tickets and had an erection just at the thought of going in. Guess what. We found Paddy with his fur coat draped over his lap happily coexisting with the best of London's perverts. A recipe for a happy life. The journey home was virtually two nights without sleep. I remember the dawn and the streams with mist rising from them. Five and a half hours journey time for what now takes under three without a high speed line. I guess we must have been on the night mail train. When we arrived home we borrowed my Dad's car and spent a day at Saltburn. We only got home with the kind generosity of home owners who filled up the car radiator on more than one occasion. Who needs sleep when you are a teenager?

Lucerne in Switzerland and up Mount Pilatus. Twice. Once In 1961 and the next time in 1998.

I was taken on a grand tour of Europe, France, Switzerland and Italy to be precise, by my mother's brother. My Uncle Ralph. Uncle Ralph wore a corset due to TB when he was a young man. I thought this happened to us all when we grew up. I loved him for his wit, his ability to draw and the attention he gave me. He was a fanatical Sunderland AFC supporter and his wish was that when his time was up, it would be in front if his team at Roker Park.

Ralph never married although he had a lifelong girlfriend called Gert who lived in London with her mother. It was their intention to marry once Gert's mother had shuffled off the mortal coil. No one realised how long the old girl would live and outlive my uncle. Ralph was nicknamed, "the sunshine boy". He loved good beer, conversation and football. So much so he went on a trip to Belgium for a Trappist beer tour in the early sixties. This was something quite special as people didn't travel much in those days. 1961 saw me drunk for the first time in my bachelor uncle's care. 9 years old and I had developed a taste for alcohol. Oh dear.

Some Other People's Lives

As I lay under stars on the hotel roof, directly opposite the funicular railway leading up to the summit of Pilatus, I slowly recovered from my first hangover. The clanking of cog on rail lives with me to this day. I was to ascend the following day with a champagne hangover and for many years wondered why we put our meat into custard before we ate it. Fondue wasn't on my radar for many years.

In remember the steep angle of the train and being asked by some American tourists, "Are you from Scotland?" I suppose the North East of England was near enough to Scotland when you're from Idaho. I was sandwiched between the Americans and the tourists being young and female, I wasn't moving. Separated from my party, I joined them at the end of the railway line before taking a cable car for the final ascent.

Nothing much has changed when I revisited 30 odd years later, except that instead of talking to Americans, I was talking to a Jewish group from Israel. All I remember them saying was, they forced us to learn English at school. The language, "breaks a my teeth". I realised how lucky I was when Uncle Ralph took me there at nine years old. The joy of visiting a foreign country isn't the country, but the people you meet, as with most events in our lives. Lucerne was and still is a magical place, the lake is beautiful and boat taxis are a great way of getting around. As with a lot of my travelling, I was away on July 4. The American symphony orchestra was playing at the lakeside auditorium and as a finale, 100 riders of Harley Davidson motorcycles beat out the American national anthem on their petrol tanks and revved their bikes in time, to the orchestration of the conductor. What a serendipitous event strongly etched into my mind.

I had to attend a meeting in Avignon, so when asked if I would attend, the answer was a resounding yes, I'll go. The journey was split between a flight from Newcastle airport and a superfast TGV train from Charles de Gaulle airport.

I'd never been on this low flying projectile of a TGV and given my love of trains, I was really looking forward to this and at sixty plus the new things you get to do in life become less and less.

The question posed, is: "When is a superfast TGV train slow?" When it hits a cow! The poppies and buttercups are filling the fields. Very beautiful, but very slow. They should be a blur of colour, not clear flowers. My opposite passenger is a Frenchman the size of the Mount Ventoux who has a terrier dog on his knee. The dog is hot and panting dog breath everywhere and I'm sure it keeps farting. I think it is the dog or god if you are dyslexic. My legs were cramping up due to lack of leg room so I went walkabout. Does this mean I'm travelling faster when I walk to the front of the train and travelling slower when walking back? Now there's a conundrum?

I have had a good chat with two meeting members who are going to Brussels first class. First class is not the same as in the UK. it just means the passengers have had a shower, unlike the second class proletariat, who still have bits of straw and mud sticking to the clothes? I noticed the coughing and sneezing is more prevalent in classe 2. Back to a work theme. The

Brussels pair put my mind at rest with regard to future research. I will avoid internal applications of bacteria to change the properties and stay with surface applications as the process is much easier. The two members were late for the meeting yesterday. They were late because the train hit a cow. I have a theory that this one farmer isn't making a living so he puts a cow on the line on a daily basis to get compensation from the rail company. I reckon they could get three impacts out of one cow. The vet is probably in on this as well, as he gets a daily emergency call out, as well as termination costs. Then there is the man with the tractor who hauls the carcass away. The Mayor of the town must have sanctioned this and he should be on 15%. French railways, a whole new way of sustaining a lifestyle. Vive la France I hear you say. I saw a sign for well tenderised boeuf.

At a knock down price. I wonder?

I've now arrived in Lyon and we can't leave the station because of a door problem. The entire population of the train have left immediately and lit up a Gitane or Gauloise cigarette on the platform. Remember the farting terrier. Even it is smoking a fag. The scene resembles something like a war movie where the refugees are allowed one last drag before deportation. A steam train would create less pollution. The platform now looks like a piano keyboard of white stubbed out cigarettes randomly strewn as if a man has attacked the keyboard with a hammer. We are underway again. Yippee.

Why the love of trains, maybe it is because of the lack of health and safety when I was a child that allowed us to wander alongside of the Sir Nigel Gresley under a head of steam in the repair yards at Gateshead. Three feet away from a massive and super powerful iron beast. You could feel the ground shake under your feet as it rolled past. How could you not fall in love with them?

Sir Nigel Gresley (Source http://www.bbc.co.uk/news/uk-england-norfolk-26416032, accessed 26.01.2015.)

Guess what I have in the loft that will not be parted from me? Tri-ang and Hornby locomotives with memories that are priceless, along with my Ian Allen train spotting books.

Retyreing at Sea

by Anon.

I glanced over at him, his blue eyes that had seen the passing of many decades still twinkling with joy, a broad grin spread across his face, and had to concede that it was, indeed, a very fine morning.

Although I was still unsure as to the reason we were out there, gently drifting around on an unusually calm sea, my habit of glancing at my watch had, at least for the moment, been suppressed.

It hadn't been a particularly *fine* morning at home. I'd got it in the neck for abdicating my responsibility for the school run, having had to be at work before seven. And it certainly was *not* a fine morning at the office when I got his 'phone call to ask me to come and meet him there. Although I would never normally have agreed to such an impromptu request, we hadn't actually seen each other since Christmas, and the lunchtime business meeting that had been arranged with a client was postponed until the afternoon. Seeing as the boatyard was en-route to that meeting, and also, I suppose, because of my realisation that my 'family commitments' conscience was somewhat battered and tarnished lately, and could do with a bit of a polish, I agreed to the rendezvous.

He'd mentioned something about him retiring at sea, and I half expected to be asked to inspect some ramshackle old vessel he'd bought, and was busy "doing up".

The morning sea mist had lifted. I stared out, sternward, in a relaxing laid back position, not from a rusty old barge bought for his retirement, but from the front of a 12 foot rowing boat. I could see the shoreline in the distance, where some people were walking their dogs on the beach. The boat rocked gently in the almost non-existent swell, and as it drifted, pivoting in a circular motion guided by the gentle, warm summer morning breeze, a horizontal panoramic 360° seamless moving picture began to take form. A vast empty sea horizon swung slowly into view. Then, as we drifted further around, a distant headland, still partly shrouded in mist, presented the skeletal outlines of huge motionless yellow cranes on a now defunct dock. Finally, as the boat completed its unhurried 360 degree drift, into view slid the two sweeping piers that formed the harbour entrance, reaching out from the land like the jaws of a vast pair of pincers, threatening to crush you as you pass between them, out of the safety of the harbour and into the now pond-like but fickle open sea.

It had been an exhausting journey. I'd rowed the whole way out, dragging a dead weight sunk below the surface on the end of a rope, straining against me from the stern in watery defiance at my every draw of the oars, but which now dangled peacefully in the quiet waters of the sea as we floated around.

The silence and serenity, except for the distant sound of a group of seagulls, was broken as he spoke again.

"I said it's a fine morning son, isn't it", he repeated, grinning and wringing his hands, not with tension or nervousness as we sometimes do in uneasy situations, but with the joy of anticipation, excitement, of good things about to happen, a characteristic he'd never lost .

"Yes. Yes, it is", I replied.

He'd always called me "son", and I didn't really mind that, I suppose. We *were* family after all. And, I also found myself thinking that I didn't really mind being out there. I was beginning to relax a little, to enjoy the scenery which changed with the circular drift of the boat; the gentle lapping of the water against the hull; the silence; the fact that I didn't really have to speak.

Silence, conversational silence that is, can be very uncomfortable socially. In all those years of socialising and social climbing, from 'A levels', through the best engineering university in the country, from one business orientated liaison to the next, to the height of my profession as the Technical Director of a successful engineering design company, that sudden abrupt halt into conversational silence was the embarrassing situation one tried to avoid. I mean, unless you're in the company of people with whom you're completely comfortable in silence, when not a word needs to be spoken; with whom, perhaps, you're "all talked out", and everything that can be said has been said and understood and gone by, as happens in a long term stale marriage perhaps, then small talk and chatter, very often nervous uncomfortable small talk and chatter, is almost a pre-requisite, regardless of its quality or its relevance. Anything to avoid an embarrassing silence.

But not now. Today, it was actually very nice for once to just lay back in a drifting boat with someone who felt the same; two people who, although due to pressures of work and family didn't see much of each other, did know each other well enough to mutually accept that silence, the easy comfortable silence, was OK.

We were on, about, our third or fourth drift around, me scanning the 360° degree pastiche from our position a hundred yards or so out from the harbour entrance, when the all too well embedded habit resurfaced, and I glanced at my watch.

"What exactly are we doing out here" I asked him.

Grandpa raised his head, revealing his blue twinkling eyes, still fixed upon a small pointed metal object he'd been inspecting since we left the boatyard. He rose up from the bench seat and turned to bend over the stern, resting his hands on the sides of the boat, still grasping his piece of metal as he peered down beneath the surface at the object on the end of the rope. Grey haired with a stubbly beard that said he was a bit too busy to shave every day, his face and neck were both weather beaten and sun burnt due to long hours spent out in the open, working in his garden. Not gardening, but working on his array of unfinished inventions and contraptions that filled almost every space of his retirement bungalow. He was tall and slim, and as he was bending over, wrists gripping the side of the boat to support himself, I noticed the odd shape of his blue jeans, hanging around his waist. The bum of the jeans hung limply were his buttocks should be. Why is it, I wondered as I looked on, that men of that age lose their buttocks, and commit the fashion faux pas of wearing blue jeans, which so clearly enhance and draw attention to this age related bodily disappearing act? I pondered on the silly notion that maybe, although not in grandpa's case, admittedly, both buttocks just retract into the body as one gets older, and then combine, pushing out to the front to form the belly that inevitably protrudes well above and outside of the old waste line of their youth.

Even at this age, Grandpa was an effervescent sort of a man, amiable, affable, everybody's friend; someone you'd find difficult to brush off if you were in a hurry and needed to get away, if you know what I mean. I'd got him a job in an engineering company I had once worked for, and he would spend his lunch and tea breaks dotting around the offices and shop floor, talking to the designers and production engineers, collecting ideas and advice, and sometimes even staying after hours to work on his latest gadget he'd smuggled on site in his duffle bag, which he slung over his back as he cycled to and from the factory. Sometimes he'd 'borrow' bits and pieces that he'd spied in the reject bin or pre-production junk pile, and which would eventually find their rightful place as part of another failed contraption at the bottom of his garden. Everyone humoured him. I humoured him.

He had taken to calling himself an *inventor* since his retirement. His retirement; yes, a tad premature. I stood back from the decision. Well, I didn't have a lot of choice really. It was an HR decision, not mine. They had told him as gently as they could so as not to hurt his feelings or risk denting his indomitable enthusiasm, that his services were no longer needed. Actually, everyone at work thought him a little bit of a nuisance, dabbling and meddling as he did, in areas that he shouldn't, to feed his latest gadget or contraption. But being one of those chippie and positive characters, he saw this imposed retirement (although he never referred to it as such) as an opportunity to spend more time "on his projects", as he put it. Nothing had become of any of them of course, even though he'd spent many many days and weeks experimenting with, one has to say, some crazy ideas and designs. Not being an educated man, he relied on mechanical instinct if you like, craft, and a little knowledge, sometimes a very dangerous thing, to fuel his ideas and devices. He was bit of a 'Toad of Toad Hall' character too; into one idea, then almost as quickly out again into something else that caught his imagination. Nothing was ever completely finished.

"What are we doing out here son?" he returned my rhetorical question, turning around again to face me, " Well, we'll see presently", a wide, knowing grin spreading over his face, causing the tight tanned skin around his eyes to wrinkle even more. He carefully placed the small piece of metal back on the bottom of the boat, folded his arms and winked one of his secretive 'all will be revealed' winks, usually a pre-cursor to a wholly predictable mechanical failure of his latest machine.

"So this is another one of your harebrained ideas you're wanting me to see, is it?" I asked, looking down accusingly at that puzzling metal object.

I had tried to moderate my disdain which must have been apparent in the way I'd asked the question, but I could see that I had stepped over the line. He unfolded his arms and slowly sat down, turning his head to stare out at the horizon so as not to meet my look.

"Grandpa", I said, with as much sympathy as I could muster, "You've had lots of ideas, but you know they've all turned out to be complete non starters. You've spent half of your life messing about with this gadget and that contraption, your so called inventions."

"That car speed indicator contraption for instance, the one that was fixed on the front bumper, and the wind was supposed to spin some disc or other and indicate to pedestrians the car's speed. Of course they had to be on top of it to read the thing. And it didn't work in the rain, or with a strong side wind.

And what about your new vertical centrifugal electric motor thing that was to change the face of transport? It certainly changed the face of your neighbour's garden when it took off over their fence and scattered their free range chickens in all directions. God knows what would have happened if it hadn't ran out of cable and yanked the mains plug out of your extension lead. Those chickens never did return to full egg production. I think the neighbours were rather reasonable and forgiving under the circumstances. Oh, and speaking of eggs, what was that automatic microwave egg poacher thing? Made a compete mess of the microwave and the kitchen. You know, grandma's had a right old time with your inventions, with bits and bobs lying around the house in various states of completion. You even use the kitchen as a test lab.

Then there was that mini crane design, for lifting stuff over garden walls. It nearly squashed the cat when it buckled and collapsed. You'd used thin scraps of aluminium from the factory, and hadn't taken into account any load calculations; nothing. It was just thrown together like a Meccano model."

Grandpa spoke in an uncharacteristically low voice, head still turned seaward. "They were good ideas" he murmured.

"Yes, but none of them *worked*. Or even got finished. I mean, you have to start with solid theory first, like the designers at the factory. You can't just make assumptions that this will work or that will work because you *think* it'll work, or that it will perform or behave like you think it will because of a guess or intuition. You are an empiricist, an experimenter. All of the modern engineering achievements are built on theory, Grandpa, which is *then* put into practice. You just can't throw things together in an experiment and expect it to work."

He turned his head quickly towards me, and I saw a flash of anger in his eyes.

"So what about the 17th and 18th century inventors and so-called scientists, they started by experimenting, with hunches, with intuition, and they built experimental models too. They didn't have the luxury of theory then, did they? They tinkered with the designs till they worked.....".

"Is that why they moved you off the shop floor then - tinkering?" I interrupted, unable to stop myself, felling the hurt of being challenged . Of course, I knew the answer. They had moved him off the shop floor because he spent too much time tinkering with the products, experimenting with the designs; all unauthorised of course. They even lost some customers. Valuable business went to competitors. So consequently he'd been 'retired' as a clerk from the office position they moved him to, and not as a shop floor technician.

"It's alright for you son, you went to public school and you had a university education. I was working class, and so was your father. We did woodwork and metalwork in my school. And when I left school, my father told me to get into a trade; a joiner, electrician, or a machine operator or something. None of us expected to learn any fancy theory. Your father gave you what we never had, never could have had. And they suffered for it, your Mum and Dad. I'll bet you didn't realise why you spent so much time with me and Grandma? Yes, of course, we loved to have you; you were great fun then, *you* would tinker around with bits and bobs then alright, wouldn't you? Anyway, things got really bad between your Mum and Dad, but they wouldn't let you see it, never let you hear the shouting and arguing. And what caused their break up? Money, that's what. They sacrificed everything for you, to help you get where you are today. It broke up their marriage in the end you know."

I didn't know.

"What are you talking about grandpa, they drifted apart, emotionally, when we left home. They had nothing in common anymore and simply split up. It happens" I said, while at the same time, rising through the undercurrents of my thoughts, I was recalling incidents that, until now, had lay unresolved in my child's mind. They avalanched into a sudden realisation that perhaps, for my well being, they may not have ever been altogether truthful with me.

"They were already apart son" he continued. "Before you left home. Your mother didn't take that low paid catering job for fun, and your father didn't change to those long night shifts for nothing, either. They just scraped through when it came to paying the bills, including your hefty school bills, while trying to put some money aside to help you out when you went to university. Yes, they managed to keep their heads above water when it came to money, but they were sinking fast in their relationship. They hardly saw each other, and it wasn't surprising that they drifted apart and 'split up', as you put it."

The boat had drifted around to the point where I could see the shoreline. It occurred to me now that the people I'd seen walking earlier were singular; they were alone, and, like subjects in a Lowry painting, their backs were bent in a effort to keep moving and upright on the dry, shifting, unstable sand; each on their own, some gazing out to the largely monotonous seascape, providing a blank canvas on which to paint their thoughts as they walked. Perhaps they were contemplating their uncertain future and wondering what, if anything, they could do to make it better. Some with heads lowered, perhaps recalling their past, Proust like, and perhaps trying to understand what went wrong, wondering where it had all gone, and what they might have done then to make it better. All of them deep in their own thoughts, stark and clear, uncluttered by external distractions, a condition that only a walk along a quiet beach can truly enable.

"And another thing" grandpa started up again "while we're on the subject of relationships, you may choose not to see it, but your marriage isn't exactly ship-shape, is it? It's plain enough to me, and *I'm* not that clever, am I son? Yes, you've got all of the visible trimmings of a successful life. Your lad is at prep. school, and no doubt you'll buy him through university. You're not short of money, are you; nice car nice house and all that. Yes, your currency account may be brimming over, but if you're not careful, *you'll* be emotionally bankrupt. You're always working, you're hardly ever home. Your work takes absolute priority. Your time is the master of everybody else's time. Don't think that I haven't noticed you glancing at your fancy watch while we've been sitting here. I'm surprised you could even afford the time to come out to meet me."

And of course, I hadn't. It was 2nd hand time that I'd afforded him, re-cycled time if you like. Time that should have been allocated to that business meeting.

So there we were, facing each other, adrift in a boat, each a single captive audience for the other's views and criticisms. Of course, we were both right. Me about his years of madcap inventions, and he about my years of neglect in my marriage. And maybe he was right about my parents' break up too. But he hadn't just brought me out here for that reason, to tell me that I spent too much time working, and that my marriage was in trouble, something I already knew but could see no way to change. No, there was another reason.

Grandpa again folded his arms, his confidence and exuberance returning, having scored a few points. He laid back on the seat, stretching out his long legs so that his feet rested in a position half way along the boat, accidentally kicking his piece of metal toward me as he did so.

"Why have I brought you out here son?". He glanced over his shoulder at that rope which dangled from the boat.

"That's why" he said, abruptly sitting up and rubbing his hands together, the grin, absent during the last few minutes of trading home truths, re-forming across his face. "I'm telling you son, I think I've cracked it this time. This *will* work, I'm sure of it. I've been thinking about this for a long time. Keep your eyes off your watch and think about *this* for a moment." He leaned stiffly farther toward me.

" How many miles of roads and motorways do you think there are in the UK son? There must be tens of thousands of miles. And how many cars, wagons, busses, motorbikes, and vans travel on them?"

"Millions" I quickly replied, trying to shorten the pre-amble, "But what's that got to do with two men drifting in a boat a hundred yards from a harbour entrance?"

"Bear with me son, bear with me. I'm getting to the point"

He'd seen the flick of my wrist, engrained within me as an unshakeable habit, as I again checked the time. I had that meeting after lunch, and I really did need to get back.

"Look" he continued, "How often do you change the tyres on your car? I'll bet it's twice a year, the mileage you do. So, work it out, millions of vehicles, millions and millions of tyres?"

He sensed my bewilderment as to where all this was leading, and he leant even farther forward, looking me straight in the eyes.

"Pass me that tyre tread depth gauge son, next to your feet."

My God, he'd even re-invented a tyre tread gauge, fashioned it out of a scrap piece of metal, the bit he'd been fiddling with since we left the boatyard. Anyone else would have spent the two quid and bought one.

He took the device from me and continued "So, what do you think happens to all of that rubber – the rubber that *was* the tread on those millions and millions of tyres, the rubber that wears off every one of them. Where is it now...where does it go son?"

I was taken aback for a moment. He was right of course. Thousands of tons of tyre rubber is constantly worn from vehicle tyres and deposited onto the roads. The stuff doesn't evaporate or disappear, and it certainly doesn't stay on the road surface.

"It all ends up here" he said emphatically, stabbing his finger downwards over the side of the boat.

"You see son, the rubber tread wears off the tyres onto the roads; the rain *must* wash it off all of the road surfaces, or we'd be up to our necks in rubber; the road surfaces drain into the ditches and culverts which drain into the rivers which flow, where?" He turned and pointed toward the harbour entrance. "Right there - tons of rubber dissolved in rainwater, flowing into the rivers and then out to sea, right under this very boat!"

"Grandpa, even if all that *were* true, I still don't understand why we are here, in the path of this...this river of rubber".

"Come on son, come on." He'd worked himself up into a state of excitement, more so because of my apparent bewilderment and inability to see his point.

"Can't you remember your school chemistry lessons? That experiment you brought home once...the crystal growing experiment. There was a blue crystal, copper sulphate I think it was, suspended on a thread in a jar full of water, which already had crystals dissolved in it, and the crystal grew and grew as it attracted the crystals that were already dissolved in the water. That's what set me thinking. *Now* do you see?"

And then it suddenly dawned on me. The simple flimsy logic of which grandpa was a master. He had come up with another completely mad and impossible scheme – to somehow collect rubber from the river water as it flowed out to sea.

"That's a tyre on the end of that rope, isn't it" I said accusingly, looking for confirmation that was even redundant in the asking - he'd already started hauling the thing up over the edge and into the boat.

"This tyre *must* attract the rubber in the water, just like the crystal in that experiment" he grunted.

I couldn't bring myself to help him. I was embarrassed for him. For this, and suddenly for all of his past failures, but mostly for this, for my absolute certainty that it would be yet another.

I raised my hands in front of my face as an old, worn out car tyre threw circular plumes of salt water spray into the air, splattering both of us with the sea water as he flung it awkwardly into the bottom of the boat.

"Look", he said, "Look at this". I sat still on my seat as he leaned forward, carefully examining the perimeter of the tyre. He rubbed the grey, wet surface here and there, pushing his makeshift depth gauge into the old cracked and discoloured rubber as he paused to examine one particular spot. "I'm sure"..he started slowly, "I'm sure...yes this has definitely got more rubber on its tread than when I lowered it into the water before we set off from the boatyard. "Definitely." he continued, looking up and grinning the usual grin at the usual pan face which I presented in these circumstances.

"Come on son", he said as he beckoned me to swap places. "I'll check it out properly when I get it back to the shed."

He rowed enthusiastically all the way back into the harbour and up to the boatyard. He glanced from side to side as he rowed, grinning all the time. He waved at some youngsters fishing on one of the piers as we passed between them, shouting "Lovely morning for it", as they stared down into the boat at its unusual, incongruous rubber cargo. Occasionally he would sporadically burst into whistling some indeterminate tune, and, every so often, he'd stop rowing and bend forward to inspect the tyre, caressing its largely bald and cracked surface with a gentle stroke of his hand, and muttering "Yes, definitely something there..."

I didn't say a word the whole way back. That long established 'easy comfortable silence' we had between us provided me with a cover for my acute embarrassment. But it was *just* the easy silence for Grandpa. There was no embarrassment. Embarrassment was something he'd lost somewhere along the way, somewhere between his early retirement and his neighbours' chickens.

"Grandpa" I called out, as he flung the wet tyre over the handlebars of his pushbike. I thought I'd better ask him. "What was it you said this morning about your retirement, about buying a boat or something."

He set one foot on the peddle and looked around at me. "Didn't listen , did you son. I'll bet you were just too busy. I said *re-tyreing* at sea, not retiring"

The penny dropped. I stared at the tyre, partly straddled between his legs, forcing them to bow out as he slowly rode away. Re-tyreing; or *re-treading,* as he should have said, wouldn't, couldn't work, and was destined to become another failure in his garden graveyard of failed and flawed ideas. Not that it would worry him unduly of course. Plenty more where that idea came from, Toad of Toad Hall and all that. The rubber tyre re-treading, or "re-tyreing" project, as he called it, would be abandoned because of some other scheme he'd dream up, and not because he would admit it didn't work. That would be too much for him to face.

"See you later son" he shouted, throwing a shaky wave of his hand without bothering to look back. He broke into whistling another indeterminate tune as he slowly gathered speed, wobbling like a child learning to ride its first bike as he made his way between dull, worn, orange crab and lobster pots stacked along the dockside. Seagulls scattered in an attempt to avoid him on his erratic path along the fish stained road and out of the boatyard. I watched him ride unsteadily through the gates and then disappear around the corner, his duffle bag slung over his back.

I stood there for a while, recalling our conversation as we sat in the boat. Not the 're-tyreing at sea' stuff, but what was said about me. About my parents, my family and my work. About my life; how he perceived it had been, how he saw it now, and how he saw it might be in the future.

But what did he know? A failed inventor.

I glanced at my watch.

A Sporting Life
by Alan Richardson

I'm sitting in the day surgery ward awaiting my op and thoughts turn to earlier days of my athletic career, now long gone. As the Greek poet Pindar inferred, sporting success is a fleeting moment in time. Nothing you can hold onto, except in your memory. How true that is now. I've just had my body mass index calculated and it is 31 – just on the obese border. Strange there are no border controls with BMI. They let anyone in!!!!!

Let us take a trip back to 1973 – I was a proper beer drinking member of society, one of the drinking classes. My waistband was expanding and I thought something needs to be done? I started with a one and a half mile jog around a local housing estate. That exercise nearly killed me; it was inspirational to my acquaintances at the time. I inspired an old alcoholic mate to join me. That was a reason to celebrate with a drink. Guess what? He was faster than me. Hang my head in shame came to mind, but if anything this spurred me on to join Durham City Harriers and this was a pivotal moment. Being beaten by a young alcoholic was bad but what was about to happen was far worse!

I was warmly greeted by a white haired old guy called Norman and he asked what my distance was? I had never really considered that question, as the sole purpose of joining the Harriers was to increase my fitness and lose some weight. Well. 200m was the distance at school that I excelled at – so 200m it was. He was old enough to be my grandfather with his white hair and white legs. I knew this was not going to be a contest, as he wore normal socks with his trainers that had seen better days. His vest was an old man's aertex vest. I was offended when he offered to give me a heads start over a 200m race, between me and a very old man. The result was not what I expected as I could do nothing about it when he sped pass me on the home straight. Half way down it to be precise.

This was a massive blow to my ego and again it provided me with compunction to raise the bar and raise my fitness.

The first few months of training were purgatory; constant aching legs did not go away. However with a year of jogging under my belt, the distance and speed improved so that an 8 mile training run could be covered in around 65 minutes – I had no idea this would come down to 45 – 48 minutes in a year or two.

So clearly – I was getting fit; milestones were passed, 10 miles in the hour, under 3 hours for a marathon etc. The winter cross country season was superseded by track races; all the while the road races were an attraction. When I say attraction, how can running so fast to make you feel sick with the subsequent pain in your limbs and tearing of the airways, be classed as an attraction. But nonetheless it was a satisfying to see an improvement in performance. I ended up training with national champions and I should have realised, I was reaching the zenith of my career, but you gain fitness so slowly, as with the weight loss, you never feel you are really fit.

Fit, I hear you say – well maybe in retrospect.

Breaking the hour for 10 miles – Croxdale, Co Durham – FA cup day.

Let me take a trip back to the Silksworth ski slope. My Sunday morning run started there. I meandered through Sunderland to the end of Roker pier, and rather than run off the end I turned around and ran back. I threaded my way back towards Silksworth and at about 14 to 15 miles into the run I passed Pallion Working Men's Club. As many successful people know, timing is everything, and this couldn't have been worse.

Dressed in Lycra running bottoms (more like women's tights), Max Wall would have been proud of me. I had two bright orange T shirts on top to complete the sartorial elegance. The only thing that was missing was Widow Twankey's make up. Although an old chap I knew from my squash club sauna days said I had a shapely leg so I must have cut quite a dash in certain parts of town? A gay on the loose comes to mind.

124

It was 10 minutes after last orders and the vomitarium exit was spewing out drunks like the Calgary stampede. As I ran past a cheer went up with ribald comments from the "real men" who drank together. Very shortly this cheer and jeering was followed by an even louder roar and presumed this was more good humoured banter. I never stopped running, as dressed like this, in this part of town could have dire consequences. I didn't realise one of the drinkers was closely following me, running in an exaggerated clown style. The cheer turned into a deafening roar as the young man overtook me and ran steadily 10 yds. ahead of me. Remember, I train with Olympic athletes, I will pass him shortly. The young man was dressed in his best bib and tucker, sporting leather soled shoes. We progressed together out of sight of the crowd. At 100m he was ahead and stayed so until 400m. I thought that's enough so I raised the pace. He turned around and responded. Guess what? I wasn't catching him. I knew I could get him because I had recently completed a 2 hour 33 minute marathon and that put me in the top 150 finishers of the London Marathon of which the top 30 or 40 were foreign elite runners. He couldn't keep that up? Could he? After 3 miles he stopped. That's it I thought, he is out of steam. I knew it but he put up one hell of an impressive performance. When you think it can't get any worse it often does.

The reality of what transpired was dreadful for a trained athlete. The only reason he had stopped was that he had arrived at his grandmother's for his Sunday lunch.

I stopped and he immediately went on the defensive assuming I was going to be aggressive with him for lampooning me. Me dressed like a gay escapee from the Bolshoi ballet, start a punch up? I think not.

I told him I was gob smacked at his level of fitness and asked him where he trained and who was his coach. A very bemused look came over him and despite our difficulty in communication, me being from a nice university town that has been a site for pilgrims for the last 1000 years – Durham, and he, with obvious speech defects, from a ship building town. We seemed to break through the communication barriers with signs, gesticulations and mutual grunts. A very primitive discussion it was, then he lit me with the bombshell when he said he was drunk and had consumed 8 pints of the club's best bitter and didn't train at all. Why would you want to if you were that fit?

He admitted he played football after this beer and after his Sunday lunch, with his friends, then returned to the club to assuage the mighty thirst that must have arisen from these considerable efforts.

What a waste, he was a World class athlete. The 'what could have been' was the case. But he didn't give a hoot about athletics.

I had my successes – 1hour 53 minutes for 20 miles at South Shields, 2 hours 33 for the London marathon, second place in the Wear Valley marathon with an 800 feet climb near the end, just missed selection for the European and Commonwealth games for the marathon and part of the winning team at Cassel, Circuit des Géants half marathon, France, but nothing compared to the beating I received from a drunk one Sunday afternoon.

The changing for cross country races involved a ritual of Vaseline between the legs and on the nipples, then vigorous rubbing of liniment onto young legs to warm them through. Fiery Jack was a liniment of real heat. The watchword is take care when going for a pre-race pee. Those that didn't could be seen leaping around doing some pagan ritual dance with a grimace on their face due to the residue from their hands.

I remember the poetry of running through woodland on a cold, crisp winter's day; there is no finer feeling when super fit, until you trip over a tree root and go arse over tit. One of my runs through Houghall wood was delayed due to a pheasant shoot comprising of beaters, dogs and guns, followed by guess what – pheasants!!!!! Dumb animals eh!!!

Athletics in Durham has a strong University group of intelligent athletes running 365 days a year as a foil to their academic endeavours. Intelligent means a better class of mischief in their case. Not for them the continuously pouring shampoo onto the head of another athlete until the entire bottle has been emptied to the narrative of, "by gum this is good shampoo you're using, look at the lather". Well of course the poor victim couldn't see because he had soap in his eyes and no matter how hard he rinsed away the shampoo it was never going to subside until the bottle was emptied. A better class of mischief meant a cruel mental manipulation of a poor, lesser mortal's mind. Athletes always worry about injury as they spend hundreds of hours fine tuning their bodies through repetition. Any perceived routine to avoid the inevitable repetitive strain injury was always worth a try. The slow of thought were convinced that by wearing a particular type of training shoe in bed, shin splints could be avoided. Not any old training shoes but an old make of Adidas Gazelle trainers (still available after all these years). Intellect is a dangerous tool when in the wrong hands!

3000m race author fourth from left. Never had enough pace for these short sprints

As the Beatles, sang, "There are places I remember all my life, but some have changed, some for better, some forever, some have gone and some remain. These places had their moments……"

Cassel France was one of those unforgettable events in my life, young, super fit and part of a GB winning team competing in a half marathon. On races days, breakfast was a very light affair so as not to inflict an upset stomach on myself due to exertion. We were met at Dover by a race organised taxi driver and we meandered our way through the French countryside, rolling hills, green field, towards Belgium and our destination, Cassel. My mind went back to the second World and First World wars. Tank battle ground topography, trench warfare fields, and flat fast countryside for my French half marathon debut. I conjured up an easy race in my mind. I asked the taxi driver how far Cassel was. He replied, "there in front of you". Where? All I could see was an extinct volcano in front of me with a toy village perched upon the top. I was dehydrated before the start of the race due to lack of liquid. You can tell I'm an educated man from that sentence? Was I hallucinating? This could not be the case. I had envisaged a flat fast half marathon. Had I been American I would said I envisioned it. We should never have allowed them independence with their headlong rush to destroy the English language. They have further faux pars such as "war on terror" – do they think we are idiots. Terror is an emotion. How can you fight emotions? Some mental institutions do? Now there's a thought?

Oh yes. Cassel. I remember now. The pre race preparation was the offering of red wine to the GB team prior to the start. I think some of the Frenchies haven't forgiven us for Agincourt. They remember the mighty English long bow and Henry V. "And gentlemen in England now-a-bed shall think themselves accursed they were not here" (apologies to Shakespeare), such was the desire to beat the other European teams. This offer of red wine was very subversive. I was prepared to act with dignity and politely refuse the alcohol remembering

Hastings 1066, there will be no repeat of that battle. Only Agincourt.

The winning team. The author, Ian Brown, Kevin French and shame on me I can't remember

The race started with a downhill charge off the volcano and I found myself in the top 10 leading group. Bugger; this downhill running kills your legs. The flat mile or so at the bottom disappeared in 5 minutes. I knew this was going to be a fast time. However, when we arrived back at the foot of the extinct volcano and saw the sign. NO COACHES OR WAGONS – ROAD TOO STEEP. I revised my plan for a fast time. Half way up the 800 foot climb I could touch the road in front of me. It was that steep. I arrived back to the village of Cassel. Just once more around the circuit I thought. Those crafty race organisers found a steep dirt track leading to the actual apex of the volcano before returning to the village. It appears to be a bit like child birth, when the woman thinks "it can't get any worse than this" then it does by a whole order of magnitude.

Oh well one last descent and yes you've guessed it another ascent. I was pleased with my time of 1 hour

16 minutes. Not fast for a flat course, but a bloody miracle on this course. Now this is where the trouble started. There was no water to drink after the race. The only possible liquid was strong Belgian lager beer or Pastis. We were declared the winning team and the Mayor of Cassel paraded us around the town, taking us from one café/bar to the next and plying us with drink. After the 20th bar the team was paralytic drunk. The race ended at 3.00pm but the party didn't finish until 3.00am in the morning. I swear to God Mark Bigourd's wife was a fairy tale princess of beauty unsurpassed. I would have run away with her at a moment's notice. Strange, I have no idea what happened to her between 3.00 am and 10.00 at breakfast. She must have time travelled for 20 years that night. Beer goggles and perception are strange bedfellows. Thank the Lord I didn't make a fool of myself. Well I think I didn't but who can say when there is drink in, there is sense out. It took me two weeks to recover from the alcohol poisoning. Oh to be that age again!!!!

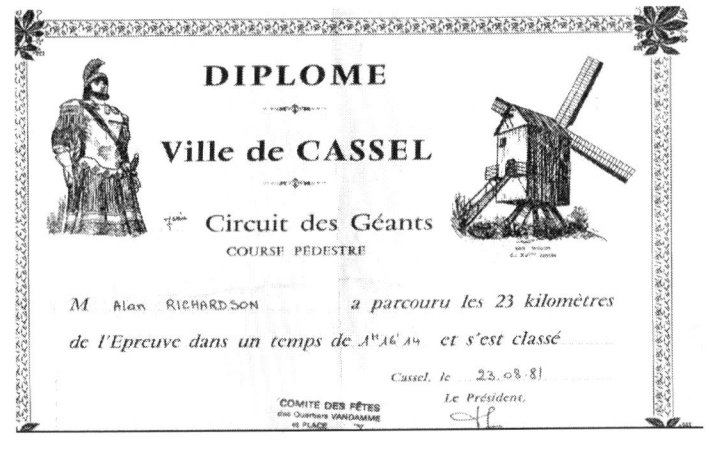

The certificate doesn't tell the full story

The National Cross Country race features six of the best club athletes from each UK running club or harriers as they prefer to be called.

Unlike modern marathons, where the organisers provide a rolling start to get thousands of athletes over the start line with a micro chip on your shoes to record the time when you start and finish, and for those less honest, intermediate times to ensure you didn't take a taxi from 1 mile out and start running again 1 miles from the finish, the National cross country race is a straight line start across a very wide field with 2000 runners standing in a straight line as you would on a track race. They are all wearing long cross country spikes as they charge headlong for a 10 yards wide gap that allows entrance to the race course.

I'm not a mathematician but I know 2000 doesn't go into a 10 yds wide gap. As a consequence of this Machiavellian organisation structure, blood is obligatory, from ankles and tendons of the runner in front. That wouldn't be too bad unless you were last, because there is someone always behind you. The key to allowing yourself a space to run in is to have the elbows out (for maximum space) and be as aggressive as possible. Prisoners are not taken. As a race, it is lethal – what happens if you fall over due to 4000 legs flapping around wildly? (For the mathematicians among us that is 2000 runners x 2 – ☺– well a mathematician would say, "How do you know they have two legs each?" "Maybe a single legged hopper, not runner?" – as the Goons would say, "how do you know someone hasn't got three?" – "are you sure it's a leg?" I can hear you say). However, if you fall, trip and unbalance due to elbows and end up on the ground, you will be peppered with long spikes by runners going flat out, nose to tail. There is no vision ahead, as the runners bodies are too close together and you are running too fast to look down. The only indication of a faller (being a runner who sadly is no longer running) is the screams he makes by being trampled on. The screams of those who fell in the "National" (cross country race) still haunt me. An uninformed (Non athletics fan and non cross country runner) bystander listening to this tale, once said, "Oh, if "you" ("You" referring to horse and jockey – not a cross country runner in a pedestrian race) fall in the National they shoot them!" This was a step too far for most hardened cross country runners. Even the long browed or five headed long armed Yorkshiremen who excel in these dangerous filthy conditions. The abbreviation of 'The National Cross Country' race to the 'National' is a dangerous change. Most housewives know of the 'National' as a horse race. Be careful what abbreviations we use. It may be the difference between life and death?

A long distance race such as a marathon is about kidology. Running flat out alongside your mate, holding a conversation and looking completely in control – nothing could be further from the truth. It is utterly demoralising to be alongside a runner looking comfortable when you are clearly not comfortable. A quarter of a mile per hour equates to a distance of three quarters of a mile on the road over a marathon. Three quarters of a mile is a huge distance to make up. This small margin is the difference between success and failure and this should be a management model when dealing with organisations that want to become winners. It is the imperceptible differences that make you a success. I remember my days as a construction director. Small things like a set of company overalls for all the staff, cleaned every week, bright shiny transport, inspirational logos, customer guarantees, all of which surround the main event of constructing a job which is to a defined quality, there is no negotiation there. Fail on this and you will not get paid and that results in bankruptcy. That is one less company to tender against. We can take a minimum standard to quality to be taken for granted, due to contractual obligations, but it is the peripheral issues that change the client's perception of you. Running and racing in particular, when you push yourself to the limit, is a learning experience that we should never forget, it is a role play situation, if you are aware enough to see the value. Most organisation run with staff that do not push themselves more than 70% of their ability and they remain successful, albeit in a less than cost effective way in terms of output and customer satisfaction. It is only on reflection that you see the value in life's experiences.

When racing, there are no margins; it is flat out until the finishing line appears. As we have seen the small differential can make all of the difference, but the question remains, which breaks first? The mind or the body?

I have been threatened with violence during a road race for kidology and not taking the race seriously. One runner put all his cards and reputation on the race, whilst moi on the other hand saw it as a day out and a chance for a bit of banter. For me there was no risk, for the other there was everything to play for. Beware of fellow competitors who have thrown in their reputation and the stakes are high. The risk of failure is a mountain too high for them. The consequences could be dire.

The story goes like this:

I ran a 1 hour 11 minute half marathon this sunny day in July. The road temperature was hot and the feet burned whilst running on the tarmac. I missed the start due to having consumed eight pints of Guinness the night before the race. Therefore my pre-race preparation was not orthodox. It was slightly reckless given the temperature the next day. I arrived when the runners were making their way out onto the course. I changed quickly and chased after them. I caught the last man after two miles of hard running on the course. I charged through the field onto the leading group after about seven to eight miles. I was flying, make no mistake, this was very fast running. It should never have been possible given my pre-race preparation. I was with the leading group of some very serious athletes when I announced I had drunk eight pints of Guinness the night before and had been out partying. I also said they shouldn't take these short half marathon sprints seriously.

It was at this point my blood would have been spilled if they could have caught me. I ran straight into the beer tent and had a social afternoon drinking four pints of the best bitter, that is once the complaint against me had been over ruled by the race committee. It was a very memorable day and my fastest half marathon despite missing the start and not taking it seriously. Is there a message in there for jobsworths and worriers?

An interesting aspect of golf courses these days is that they are littered with old people called friends, all with knackered knees, hopeless hips and failing flexibility. Guess what? They were all ex runners, ex squash players or ex some savage activity that wears the joints out. This makes playing golf a pleasure as I reminisce with my old mates, when nothing else is possible other than writing about it.

The skiing community have had après ski evenings as a key component of their sport. All athletic evenings were completed by swilling Samuel Smiths beer before returning home. In the pub the training was reviewed, future outings planned both athletic and social, epic coach journeys were relived. Indeed if we had a league match away or a major event that required a coach, we would often stop at Wetherby for some beer. It was food to the hungry and drink for the thirsty. Often more thirsty than hungry? After the National cross country at Round Hay Park near Leeds there was the obligatory stop at Wetherby to take on board beer, lots of it. After all they had been on the coach for at least 20 minutes!!!!! I had been working in Keighley for the days preceding the race so they came south on a coach and I drove East to meet them at Round Hay Park. The cross country race was fairly uneventful with the top names cleaning up with the top places. I sat and chatted to Chris who was divorced at the same time as me, therefore we were both rejected miserables together. He had run poorly at the cross country race and was a little depressed. On the other hand I was quite enjoying my new-found enforced freedom. I supported him and encouraged him to see the positive side of life (Alan the eternal optimist). I told him to shed the concept that people didn't care about him, that he was a key player in our team, very true for me because it was Chris's pacemaking that got me my fastest 20 mile time. He was a mate we went drinking with, running three times every week and had days away at races. Chris could always be relied upon to be drunk, so much so, after staying at my house after a wild Saturday evening. A large glass of my Mount Gay Rum was sitting on the work bench and he downed it before a 20 miles Sunday morning run. In his own words, this was fantastic and he should include this as part of his daily training regime! Mount Gay Rum, now there's name for a training drink? Mount gay – does that keep you fit. Ask Freddie Mercury. He might disagree! No more mounting gay or otherwise in this story. Back to the depression surrounding Chris. I had four bottles of Worthington's White Shield beer, as I reckoned my pint sized bladder could hold two pints for the journey home. Chris had consumed four pints; clearly he had the bladder of a horse. Nothing else of one as I should know given the communal showering arrangements. I eventually raised his spirits from a Churchillian black dog to plain depressed when we drained our glasses and walked to the foyer where the coach was waiting over the road for the passengers/athletes boisterously talking their way from the pub. I wished him well and arranged to meet up for a training run, now let's recount the problem of no one caring about him. Dismissed with vim and vigour with my optimism. As he walked across the road to the bus it pulled away without him, leaving him speechless in the middle of the road.

Not to worry I was at hand and gave him a lift home. Remember these were the pre mobile phone days. If you wanted to contact someone, they had to be in a house and you had to find a telephone box. Instead of having a happy ending it has an unhappy one. No one missed him until they were nearly home and the bus had to turn around and try to find him. Of course they couldn't find him as I had taken him home. No one reported him missing to the police; no one rang me to see if I had given him a lift. He was quite correct; no one gave a hoot about him. Well maybe I did and still keep in touch to this day. He thought, that afternoon, "could life get any worse than this?" Well sure as hell it did later in the day. I remember to quote an old friend called Josie, "When one door closes, the next generally jams your fingers". Never a truer word from one of life's characters; that we need more of rather than less. If you are judged by your family as an embarrassment then you are probably doing it right.

Finally, it was a Northern league match in Wallasey near Liverpool. I headed the 5000m race until I blew up after six laps. A lad called Malcolm Prince was the 5000m star of the day, he competed head to head with Steve Cram who went on to do amazing things with his career. You will gather from this, the competition was fierce. On the coach journey home, boys will be boys and each member of the team was semi stripped of their clothing until it came to me. I was the last victim so I had a special treat. They stripped me nearly naked (bar underpants) and held me up on the back window of the coach, displaying my wherewithal to the vehicles behind and the ones overtaking. Eventually I recovered my dignity and I was given my clothes back.

I'll leave you with this one final thought. When calling in at the petrol station later that week, the girl behind the counter said, "You'll never guess what we saw on the way back from York".

My reply was, "It was me!!!!"

Thirty Three Years before the Mast with Narcotics
by David Wood.

By narcotics I don't mean anything illegal but for a large part of my life, before I gave it all up for violin-playing and fly fishing, I was a Consultant Anaesthetist and I must have administered thousands of legitimate narcotics to other people. However, I'll say the word again because it always causes a bit of confusion ... ANAESTHETIST.

First you have to learn how to say it: AN - EESTH - E - TIST. Its roots are in ancient Greek (from the days when the Greeks could afford to give stuff away, even if it was only words) and it's built from "<u>an</u>", meaning absence of, and "<u>aisthesis</u>", meaning sensation. It isn't pronounced "aneethertist" or "aneefertist". It has nothing to do with aesthetics, which means beauty. An absence of beauty among anaesthetists would be, well...unthinkable.

Of course there were no anaesthetists until about 1840 so the word is, in one sense, manufactured. In the USA, where they have absolutely no sense of history before George Washington, they don't have anaesthesia. Instead they have anesthesia. Notice the crude difference? Still in the USA, an "anesthetist" isn't actually a doctor; it's a nurse who gives anesthesia, usually but not always, under the supervision of an "anesthesiologist" who *is* a doctor. This is how Americans love to screw up their word roots. And they don't even pronounce it properly.

In the UK all anaesthetists are qualified and registered doctors. They've been through five years of medical school, and then at least one year of hospital medicine and surgery at trainee level. Specialist training in anaesthesia begins at some time after that and takes a further period of at least six years before it is possible to apply for a consultant post. I was once asked by a patient if I'd had to go to night school to be an anaesthetist! I suppose, on reflection, I *had* gone to night school, given the amount of time spent in the hours after midnight in various hospitals.

Incidentally, in following my traditionalist (*i.e.* Luddite) tendencies I refuse to refer to patients as anything but "patients". They're not "clients" in my vocabulary and never will be - so there.

Most people manage to get through life without actually knowing what an anaesthetist does. The image of the bloke with the ether-soaked cloth or the big black rubber mask should have been consigned to the history books by now.

So should the character portrayed by Richard Gordon in his "Doctor in the House" book, namely, the one at the head end of the operating table who, when not actually asleep himself, was engrossed in the Telegraph crossword. One of my fellow trainees in 1972 was a Doctor Sleep. I often wonder if he ever made it in anaesthesia. And, come to think of it, I did once know an anaesthetist who spent a sizeable proportion of his operating theatre time on the 'phone to his bookmaker (and this was long before mobile phones were available).

I suppose he *was* Irish, from County Cork, so that doesn't count.

Also, when I've made reference to "himself" and "bloke" I should point out that nowadays, just as about half of the population are women, the same ratio applies in medicine and anaesthesia.

The 21st century anaesthetist has diversified into other branches of medicine, although the process of sending patients to sleep (and waking them up again) so that surgery can be carried out is still a major part of life. Anaesthetic techniques have become ever more sophisticated, as have the methods of physiological monitoring of patients whilst they are "under". A finger on the pulse and a blood pressure cuff on the patient's arm are no longer sufficient, and rightly so.

In fact an increasing number of operations are carried out under regional anaesthesia, which includes epidural and spinal techniques together with an array of other major nerve blocks. This means that unconsciousness is not always required, especially if it is unsafe in some patients. That's not to say that a degree of sedation cannot be added to these techniques. A little intravenous "Valium" or similar makes it less likely that a patient will remember the in-theatre jokes!

As well as working in the operating theatres, you will find anaesthetists in charge of Intensive Care units (which I was for a number of years), running clinics for patients with chronic pain problems, providing pain relief services to mothers-to-be in labour and performing a crucial role in hospital resuscitation teams. It always amuses me that when viewing popular TV programmes like "Casualty", it's rare to see an anaesthetist. If one is 'sent for' they're usually given a non-speaking background role. Maybe an Equity card is not required.

So that's got the dreary background stuff out of the way. Having spent, as I say, in excess of thirty years in that previous life, I've tried to remember a few anecdotes of a suitably entertaining nature. Obviously some aspects would not be suitable for this publication. Life in the world of intensive care and trauma always has its fair share of sadness and tragedy.

One of my early triumphs was the successful introduction of background music into our local operating theatres. I had first seen this in action when I was still a medical student and I'd arranged a temporary summer attachment to a hospital in Bromsgrove, Worcestershire. The hospital has long gone now, so I feel pretty safe in mentioning it. In this hospital was a surgeon who played the piano and an anaesthetist who played cello. They would play sonatas together at home then bring a tape recording into theatre, whereupon they would criticise each other's playing. Often it was quite peaceful, sometimes it became quite heated. I never saw anything thrown though. An airborne scalpel can be a frightening ballistic weapon.

As a Consultant my usual Thursday operating list would begin at 8.30am (honest!) and would often not finish until 9pm. So to soothe any fevered brows in the theatre I acquired an old audio cassette player and made up a few tapes. Now it's true to say that any tape or disc labelled as "miscellaneous" should be viewed with healthy suspicion. Whatever is on it is guaranteed to displease somebody, although I tried to keep it fairly bland. The senior theatre sister (and when I say "senior" I mean *very* senior) made it quite clear that she disapproved of this young kid with his fancy ideas about music. But the surgeon was in favour, so she had to keep her mouth shut. I decided to make up a new tape just for her containing a track by Ian Dury and the Blockheads which really was entitled "Fucking Ada". Those two words were all that the chorus contained, and they were repeated over and over. She was the only person in the room who pretended not to notice and neither did she pass comment on the sniggering that was going on. She didn't say much for the rest of the day though.

I'm not sure if the Law of Unintended Consequences had been described in those days, but my musical revolution very nearly came badly unstuck on one occasion in the gynaecology theatre. It was nearly Christmas and I had a selection of quiet Christmassy music playing in the anteroom. I won't say what operation the young girl patient was awaiting but I suddenly remembered what the next track on the tape was going to be; Johnny Mathis singing "When a Child is Born". I leapt onto the stop button in the nick of time. Let me just say that it would have been a highly inappropriate choice of music.

Towards the end of my career I worked with a surgeon (he's still around, so no names) who loved to have loud "heavy metal" music in his theatre. It used to drive me round the bend. My great musical revolution had turned around to bite me.

A few lines back I mentioned the spectre of the big black rubber mask. One huge advance (apart from the invention of clear plastic and silicone) was the introduction, in 1989, of a device called a laryngeal mask. This was a British invention produced by one Dr. Archie Brain who eventually sold the patent, retired happily and his laryngeal mask is now in use worldwide. When in place it looks just like an end of the well-known endotracheal tube protruding from the patient's mouth. Obviously the patient has to be already asleep before it can be inserted, and that sleep is achieved with an intravenous injection. The business end of the laryngeal mask is best described as being like a cup with an inflatable rim, made out of latex, (they're now made from silicone because of fears of latex allergy). The cup sits in the back of the mouth, covering the opening of the larynx (voice box) and the patient can breathe normally during general anaesthesia whilst the anaesthetic mixture, which is usually air/nitrous oxide/oxygen in varying amounts plus a volatile anaesthetic vapour, is breathed in (and out) through the tube part. Thus the anaesthetist is spared the chore of sitting for hours on end hanging on to a face mask and has his or her hands free for important monitoring and recording tasks. Please cast all thoughts of Telegraph crosswords from your mind.

The original description by Dr. Brain was that during recovery the laryngeal mask should be left in place until the patient is sufficiently conscious to remove it him (or her) self. You might think this sounds awful but if you've ever had a general anaesthetic you will know that you probably don't even remember being in the recovery room, even though to a casual observer you appear to be awake. On one occasion a lady with one of these devices still in place was in the recovery room when she suddenly sat up, wrenching the large latex end from her mouth with the words "Stop it, John. It's not time for that!"

And so to the subject of anaesthesia for dentistry. It's a subject in which I hadn't developed any special interest but in about 1981 the Durham Community Dental Service persuaded one of my colleagues and me that there was a real need for general anaesthesia for tooth extractions among thousands of County Durham kids who had had little or no dental care. I'm sure that we can all remember our childhood anaesthetics at the dentist. If you are of a certain age then it is highly likely that the anaesthetic was given by the dentist himself. You probably weren't given a lot of oxygen - certainly not the 21 percent present in normal room air. Most of it was nitrous oxide ("laughing gas"). Then the dentist would snatch a few teeth out whilst you started to recover from what was essentially asphyxia. Every year in England and Wales four or five otherwise healthy children did not manage to survive this insult given in the less than ideal surroundings of backroom dental surgeries with no other staff than the dentist and an unqualified receptionist / clerk. The only thing that eventually changed this situation was not the threat of litigation, whether realised or not. It was the refusal of the then Dental Estimates Board to pay the dentist if a second person was not named as the anaesthetist. Money has always talked!

Even then the situation was not ideal, since the "anaesthetist" was not required to have any relevant training other than the five or so anaesthetics which he or she had given under supervision as a medical undergraduate twenty or more years previously. Various government reports prompted very sluggish improvements in the situation.

So in about 1982 I took on some Friday morning sessions in what was known as chair dental anaesthesia, in various clinics and dental surgeries around the county. Much of the time their safety equipment was minimal so I supplied my own and lugged it all around these places. In twenty years though, I never had to use any of it. Although at least I knew what it was all for, unlike most of the part-time dental anaesthetists who I came across. Apart from three general dental practice surgeries in Durham, and one Community dental clinic, I experienced the delights of surgeries in such places as Peterlee, Wingate, Blackhall, Easington, Seaham, Monkwearmouth, Stanley and Chester-le-Street. It's not hard to see, when travelling around these places, why dental neglect happens. Now (2015) it's on the increase again, and not just in County Durham. It's apparently becoming a national problem once more and it cannot be of no significance that many dentists stopped their NHS work ten or so years ago when they failed to negotiate satisfactory contract payments.

The vast majority of these chair dental cases then were children and I always enjoyed the challenge of treating frightened children properly and kindly. I include hospital work in that statement. I hated dealing with the occasional "dental" adult and regarded that as so unnecessary. But there is one "category" of patient which doesn't fit either group. By this I mean patients with special needs - that's the current term but it changes from time to time depending on the prevailing fashion.

I can still recall my first special needs dental case - in a dental hospital 300miles away from Durham. I was very much a trainee working with an experienced Consultant Anaesthetist. The patient was a young man with Downs Syndrome who clearly had no intention of letting anyone near him. Today, if persuasion didn't work, he would be sent away again because he would be regarded as being over the age of consent, even if he was in fact incapable of giving valid consent (or, for that matter, withholding it). In those days the niceties did not prevail and it was my job, with the help of a couple of porters, to hold him down. Good plan, except that he was running around. We managed to get hold of him and wedged him with one arm caught between the double doors through which he had tried to escape. On the other side of the doors was my senior colleague, armed with a large syringe. He was a pretty slick operator and we heard him call out "Right, catch him" as the Pentothal went up the vein. I had never realised until then that someone could suddenly become so heavy! But we managed to heave his unconscious body onto a trolley to allow the rest of the treatment to proceed.

Years later when I now regarded myself as having a certain expertise in this sort of work, we had managed to set up a system in County Durham in the old maternity theatre in Shotley Bridge Hospital which meant that patients with special needs could have a much improved dental anaesthesia service in surroundings which we managed to make fairly non-intimidating. On a regular basis, with the less cooperative patients, we would co-ordinate with Community Chiropody and hairdressers, so that the really difficult-to-manage patients could have their hair cut and their nails trimmed whilst under the same general anaesthetic for dentistry!

All that has gone now, in the name of progress. Nowadays, frightened children and even more frightened patients with special needs have to be treated in the really scary surroundings of our general hospitals. It's supposed to be "safer", whatever that means, although the statistics do not necessarily support this. It's certainly become more difficult to deal with large numbers of patients. You'll have noticed, dear reader, that I'm not guiltless when it comes to biased opinions!

One incident which I hesitate to recount, because it could have got me into trouble, although it was now quite a time ago, was at Monkwearmouth Dental Clinic in Sunderland. Sunderland, as many people know, has a large but excellent centre for autistic people, and I have to confess that I always found autistic people very difficult to deal with. They are usually far more intelligent than average, and don't like the sort of patronising baby-talk which so often comes out of the mouths of hospital staff. One of the centre's young adults was brought along for dental treatment under general anaesthesia but, since he refused to get into the chair, had to be sent away again. I gave the carers an envelope containing two tablets of Valium and rebooked his appointment for the following week, with an instruction to give him the Valium two hours before he came back.

At the appointed time one of the carers came in and said that, despite the Valium, he was now refusing to get out of the car! I wasn't having a very good day, and really didn't want him to waste another hour of appointment time so I asked them to bring the car around to the (ground level) fire door which was in the back street. The dental nurse and I took a wheelchair, some more Valium and a few safety items down the ramp and met the car. The patient was in the front passenger seat of a Ford Escort and was probably a bit distracted by the bin lorry squeezing past on the other side of the car! Before he knew what was happening, I'd slipped an IV cannula into a vein and made him "cooperative" with Valium. We heaved him out of the car, into the wheelchair and ran back up the ramp into the surgery where he was duly plonked into the chair and treatment was completed successfully. I think that if the General Medical Council had been aware of all this they would have had something to say. My defence would have been that occasionally, just occasionally, it is necessary to fly "by the seat of the pants".

Although I'm nearly running out of stories with an anaesthetic slant, one thing which I would say is that patients presenting for general anaesthesia seem to have three main worries:

1. That they won't wake up again

2. That they won't actually be asleep when they're supposed to be, and / or

3. That they'll be sick afterwards.

It seems to me that (1) and (2) are mutually exclusive. My last look at national statistics (more than 10 years ago) suggested that mortality due to anaesthesia alone is something like 1:350,000 administrations. I don't know that valid statistics exist for (2).

The subject of (3) is interesting. The problem now is certainly far less than it was in the days of ether and chloroform. Modern drugs and anti-emetics have seen to that. But the causes of vomiting after surgery still form a list which would go to several pages, and most of them are not anaesthesia-related. And women are much more likely to suffer than men. But in children, it's the boys who are more prone than the girls. I've never been able to figure out at what age the sex-difference is the same.

But the apocryphal stories from dental surgeries continue. In the 80s and 90s when every child walking into a dental surgery seemed to be wearing either a shell suit or a track suit I grew to be very wary of chubby 10-year-old boys wearing track suits which had the trade name, "ASICS", embroidered onto the material. It usually meant that they would be, and that a catching dish should be kept to hand.

Whenever I see anyone wearing that embroidered name, even today, my mind goes back to a little upstairs back-room dental surgery!

It Started with a Kiss
by E Langley De Montfort

"It started with a kiss". Well, that's what Errol Brown, the late lead singer of 'Hot Chocolate', would have been blasting out of the disco PA at the Butlins Clacton holiday site in the late 1980s, had it not closed down in 1983 due to cheap and bloody awful package holidays, greater disposable income for the masses, and a more enlightened attitude from B&B owners to couples who just wanted to spend days in a theme park and nights shagging in a 'chalet' the size of a dog kennel and the ambience of a bloody KGB cell.

We four friends stayed at a few Butlins sites in the late 60s and 70s.

Getting up from a beer-stained table in our local pub in 1971, it did start with a kiss, French-air-kiss style, as we bade goodbye to the two girls. French-air-kiss style because they weren't our girlfriends and their perturbed boyfriends were already envious of our previous girlfriend adulation inspiring antics. We parted promising to report back, with photographs, confident of the fun and adventure to be had at Clacton. We were very cocky, and very wrong, and we were 'had'. However, as a result of this misinformed decision to spend a week at one of the most boring Butlins sites in the world, where the most stimulating bit of action turned out to be an elderly lady being pronounced a finalist for 'Glamorous Grandmother of the Week', we found ourselves driving into central London in an attempt to ward off insanity by way of a bit of adventure.

All four of us had looked on in envy at the scene from the Beatles' film 'Let it Be' when, on January 30, 1969, the Beatles held an impromptu performance on the roof of Apple Corps' studios at no. 3 Savile Row, and wished we had been there, particularly to see a group of London 'rozzers' (policemen) appear on the roof, attempting to stop the concert 'from interfering with Londoners' business and lunch breaks'! Poor things. Well this week *we* were going to be paying an impromptu visit to that very spot, and bringing back the absolutely necessary photographs to prove it.

We parked the van, with its cargo of Mum's oranges, the feather mattress, banjo et al, up near Highgate and made our way to Regent Street.

Now, sneaking into buildings where we lived was never a problem. We knew our city and pretty well its buildings' layouts, but this one turned out to be a little more difficult, as Savile Row is on a terrace with no visible rear entrance, and the buildings in the immediate area are large blocks of conjoined terraces. The main reception entrance, the only obvious entry point, was manned by a security goon, his sole raison d'être and possibly his only life achievement being to prevent the crowds of groupies and other oddballs who constantly gathered there from entering the building, Beatles protégé bands and hangers-on excluded.

We managed to jostle our way to the front and up the steps, peering into the small reception area with its posh desk, wall coverings and expensive decor, completely compromised by the Big Security Bloke. We weren't going to get past that. We chatted for a while to the small crowd, descending back onto the street to consider the challenge. It turned out that they'd been hanging around there for days, some hoping to catch a glimpse of a Beatle, or any of the famous and not so famous Beatles protégés and wannabe folk who'd been befriended by and might benefit from the largesse of the Apple Corps brand, some of the bystanders waiting there for more dubious purposes. I suppose we'd just swelled that lot's numbers by four.

The only possible way in was obvious to us. The very rooftop exit stairs from which the Beatles, Billy Preston et al had ascended onto the roof from the studios below. The problem was that *we* somehow had to get onto the roof area of that very large block of terraces via another nearby building so we could descend those stairs.

Kent & Curwen now occupy number 2 Savile Row, however, it was Gieves & Hawkes high-class tailoring business that occupied these premises at the time, and who welcomed us into their hallowed halls.

"How do you do Sirs.." was the slightly surprised, measured but unexpectedly polite response to four scruffs walking brashly through the front door of one of the best and certainly one of the most exclusive tailors in London. We wore tattered blue jeans, T-shirts and had long hair that John Lennon would have been proud of, but the guy didn't bat an eyelid or change his demeanour toward us. There was a lot of rich hippy looking people wandering around London at the time, and one couldn't risk alienating them by an indiscretion or a misjudgement of their social or wealth status.

"Can one help one?"

"No thanks; one is merely searching for access to the roof area, my man." was my reply.

"Very well sir."

Crazy.

He watched, in quite a kindly and unperturbed manner, as we marched on up the stairs to discover that there wasn't a roof access point. We even went into the top floor toilets, where I clambered clumsily out of the window, but to no avail. A hefty metal mesh structure, and failure, stared us in the face.

The building on the other side of number 3 was our next bet, and so to the beautifully delivered comment of *"Perhaps we could help one on Sir's next visit?"* we sauntered out of High Class Suit World and headed past the groupies along to, what was at the time, the London HQ of Max Factor.

It was easy. No reception, just a nice hall with lifts into which John, Fin, Neil and I walked, pushing the top floor button as we grinned at each other. We were joined at the penultimate top floor by two very smart women who eyed us up and down, but asked no questions. As I said, there was a lot of rich hippy looking people wandering around London at the time, and security was incredibly lax. These days you couldn't get away with any of the stuff we did. Reaching the top floor, as we eagerly walked out of the lift and espied an open staircase that we thought might lead up to the roof area, the women strode off gracefully in another direction, not giving us a second glance.

At this point, Neil did an about turn, and the last we saw of him till later that afternoon was his rather earnest face disappearing behind sliding doors as he said *"You three just go up. I've got to make an important phone call"*. We glanced at each other knowing that he didn't know anybody with a bloody phone, important or not, and that, not for the first time, he'd chickened out of an adventure.

How would he manage to turn that around when we next met the girls in the pub? He managed.

Neil was an odd character. I was first introduced to him as I sat one evening in a Wimpy bar before catching a late train to London to see the Motor Show at Earls Court, that wonderful building which, by the way, in the manner of what they would have done with St Pancras station had it not been for Sir John Betjeman's campaign, is now scheduled to be demolished to make way for more housing and more bloody desperately-needed-my-arse shops and offices to feed the rampant capitalist monster. Is there a modern Betjeman who'll take on the bloody capitalist developers and get the building listed?

As Neil and I had met for the first time that night, protocol demanded we exchange our views on bands and music, which identified, amongst others, the Beatles as having common appeal. Neil, in an embarrassing attempt at currying favour, seized on what he felt was a potentially endearing compliment. He loudly announced to me, whilst unashamedly directing it at the other customers as they hunched over their plates and munched on their burgers and Wimpy Benders, "..*you so so much resemble Paul McCartney, Edwin*". Looks passed between us 'Three' who were well aware of my strikingly un-McCartneyesque features, while everyone else in the place stopped munching and looked up to see a Paul McCartney un-lookalike staring silently and blankly at Neil's convincingly sincere grinning face.

I later wondered, although Neil was both odd and persuasive, how he'd managed to soft- soap John into introducing this neighbour of his, who then managed through his manufactured charm to ingratiate and inveigle his way into our group as the 'Walter Mitty' of the Four.

Neil wanted to be liked and accepted at all costs, which necessitated him concurrently inhabiting both reality *and* his completely self-fabricated ethereal world, from where, what he wanted to believe or needed to believe was real, was extracted and layered like a decoupage of lives onto the real tangible world *as* reality, to be silently tolerated without question. So no-one challenged his McCartney assertion. Not to his face, anyway, and while many of his attempts at being accepted were forgivable, some even possibly having some basis in reality, many where patently not. For example, he'd invented a middle-eastern-princess-wife, met while working in a hotel, to bolster his manliness and success with women, and to soften the harsh reality of loneliness, and when we foolishly and quite innocently indicated we'd like to meet her, Neil announced only days before the proposed get-together that she'd tragically died in a car accident in Norfolk. No-one dies in car accidents in Norfolk; the bloody roads are so bad you can't drive faster than 20 mph.

Such was Neil's assured, persuasive conviction in living out this dual existence that we three who knew his condition accepted him as a sad and pathetic amusement. However, we all loved him, with his faults and his sad vulnerability, because that latter 'attribute' was one most of us were painfully familiar with in our childhood. So we put up with him and he came with us on most adventures. But not this one.

John, Fin and I continued on to quickly climb the stairs we'd spotted, which indeed led out onto the Max Factor roof area. It was only a few steps later, taking in the wonderful sunny rooftop vista of London, that we stood where the Beatles had played, peering into the open door that led down to the studios. Yes!

We needn't have worried about being discovered and exposed as roughly dressed hippy interlopers; there were dozens of the buggers milling around on the lower floors as we descended the stairs. We had just sat on a comfy antique sofa when a pretty young thing passed and asked if we'd like some tea. Very sweet, seeing as we were in a place with perhaps the largest mobile stock of Class A, B and C pocketable drugs in London. Declining the offer and realising that, looking the way we did, we probably wouldn't be challenged anywhere once inside the building, we set off to explore it.

The next hour or so saw us delving into many rooms and recording areas, looking for photo opportunities and booty to take as souvenirs and proof to the girls that we did actually do the deed we'd so brag about as we sat opposite them and their glowering boyfriends in the pub back home. There was a number of framed Gold Disc awards on the walls of one room, and it would have been so easy to let 'sticky fingers John' shove one down his pants, but I managed to persuade him that it was at the very least immoral, so he, Fin and I settled for a number of song sheets, taking an extra few for Neil to evidence and assist with his inevitable convoluted assertion to the girls that he was definitely really there with us amongst it all.

Presently, we made our way unchallenged to the ground floor and found the main reception area, the security goon standing outside on the steps looking down over the crowd. His broad back and bald head were visible as he enjoyed his rare assertion of power entertaining the delicious hippy girls who drooled on his every word as he told of past visits by the Fab Four, and proffered the possibility that one or all of them might arrive at any minute.

We took this opportunity to photograph one another sitting at the desk, telephone in hand, before politely easing past the goon and dramatically diverting all attention to us as the throng were suddenly presented with the reality that we had managed to sneak into the Savile Row HQ of Apple Corps.

The abandoned goon, forsaken of all attention, glumly returned to the reception desk, doubtless racking his brain as he tried to recall the name of the band whose rag-tag hippy members had just left the building. We, however, were heroes, smothered with fawning adulation from worshipers who loosed off a babble of concurrent questions as to how had we done it and *"did you see or meet any bands?"*. A dubious character who candidly announced he was a record Bootlegger offered us untold fabulous riches if we'd guide him to the recording tapes. Of course we didn't divulge anything to anyone, forever guaranteeing us the status of awesome gatecrashers; reverse-Houdinis who were able to escape *into* impossibly impenetrable fortresses.

Neil had rushed from the other side of the street to jostle for position next to us, just in time to bathe in some of the kudos we'd attained, ironically declining to comment and waving his hands dismissively at the crowd as they excitedly fielded direct questions about the amazing event in which he hadn't actually participated.

The crowd were still pleading for more tales of the episode as we, like kings dismissing their courtiers and withdrawing to their more considerable and important activities, withdrew from Savile Row and headed off to complete one more mission; to pose for a photo on the famous Abbey Road zebra crossing in St. John's Wood, and to sneak into EMI's Abbey Road studios, where we would deliver our three minute 'Farting Shitting Toilet Tape' to George Martin, marked for his immediate attention, production and release as that year's weirdest, funniest and most unlikely top ten hit.

An outrageous and totally off-the-wall idea had occurred to me that just might make us famous as 'one hit wonders' without singing or playing instruments, in a conventional manner anyway. I had a cassette recorder, complete with an external microphone, and one of Liam's musical farts let loose one evening in the students union building was accidentally recorded, plunging us into fits of childish toilet humour laughter.

I suggested that we all contribute to a recording. A three-minute recording which we would offer to a publisher in protest at the crap that we perceived was crawling out of the ashes of the late sixties. And the irony was that our offering was crap as well, literally, although it turned out to be quite musical; a recording of some of our farting and shitting episodes, recorded in our own toilets, with the microphone hanging at the rim of the bowl. Liam was, predictably, cock-a-hoop at this idea, and laid down the first track. We'd each take the equipment into the 'little room studio' when the call presented itself, record the number two or attempted number two deeds, then pass the equipment on to the next in the group, having all agreed absolutely not to review what we'd each recorded.

We laughed so deeply we could hardly draw breath or stay sitting upright on the night of the premier, which took place in my bedroom. The continuous and contiguous three minute recording of straining, farting, which included the squeaking, rasping and booming kind,

Some Other People's Lives

the plopping and sploshing, had us all in fits of uncontrollable laughter, almost unable to breathe. We may have been in our early twenties, but we were helplessly overcome with this audio toilet humour.

We listened to it over and over again. I made a copy and kept it in a Jiffy bag in the van , and it was soon to be presented in person to EMI

Fast forward to Savile Row, some time later.

Unfortunately, we hadn't reckoned on the sheer adoration, respect and esteem bestowed upon us by the folks on the steps of 3 Savile Row. Turning around, we were confronted, like Brian in Monty Python's 'Life of Brian', by a gaggle of acolytes announcing with religious fervour that they just had to come with us to Abbey Road. How had they found out? The kudos seeking Neil, whom I realised I had seen knowingly winking as he did so, had 'confidentially' told one of them.

"You can't come. We'll lose the element of stealth. How do you think twenty plus people are going to sneak into a place like that?" I pleaded, without even listening for a response as we turned and strode ever more quickly along the street.

We couldn't shake them off and so we all eventually arrived in force at the famous zebra crossing featured on the 'Abbey Road' album cover, where one of the acolytes readily agreed to photograph the four of us emulating the Beatles. I wonder how many fans had been photographed striding across those hallowed tarmac black and white street-piano keys?

We reasoned with the horde, in an attempt to effect a successful sneak-in to the studios, that they should wait at the entrance 'til we had delivered the tape and at the same time carried out a quick reccie. They hung around outside, pushing against the entrance doors and craning to see in through the glass as we put the tape on the counter, not believing our luck at there being no-one at reception. Grasping the opportunity, we quickly walked through some doors, out of site of our followers, who, worrying that we had abandoned them, and seeing no personnel to stop them, tumbled noisily through the main entrance and followed us via the doors that, swinging slowly shut behind us, had revealed our direction.

There was an almighty altercation at the tail end of the acolyte crocodile as it was apprehended by some goons. Just as we were about to enter one of the studios, we were also intercepted and escorted out of the building, protesting *"We're here to see George. George Martin, that is, not Harrison."*. As the number of goons increased, we realised we had been thwarted by the very people who'd blindly and foolishly trusted us to repeat the Apple Corps Studios stunt. We never said we'd do it with them, though.

We all parted on reasonably good terms as fans of pop idols do, and we headed back to sunny Clacton to the risk of finding ourselves somewhere near an epic 'Glamorous Grandmother' final, and to have the camera film processed, so providing the ultimate proof of mission accomplished; except perhaps for Neil. Perhaps.

"Neil, how come you're not on any of these Apple studio photos then?" was the question that hung not unlike the Sword of Damocles over Neil's head as we sat sipping our Watneys Red Barrel in the pub back home, the photographs being passed around the girls and their covetous boyfriends.

"Ah..." says Neil, doubtless convincing himself, ever more strongly now in the face of interrogation, that he was actually on the mission, *"I took all of the photos, so I wouldn't be on them, would I?"*.

Having then quickly produced the 'proof' as he pulled from his pocket a couple of song sheets which had appeared in the photographs, Neil was never challenged again, and we three didn't ever positively assert that Neil *hadn't* been with us, although the lack of affirmation that he *had* was sufficient to confirm the real truth of the matter to those who knew him, and knew of the dual realities in which he co-existed.

Neil didn't come with us on the next visit to London, which we'd arranged a week later, we deciding to really show off and do a repeat of the great Savile Row sneak-in. This was despite the risk of us being late back home to attend a very promising party that was being held at our friend Titch's house, adjacent to the police station at which his father worked.

So, in tempting fate, we embarked on another adventure, one which didn't quite turn out how we'd expected it to.

Parking the van at the same venue as last time, we arrived at Savile Row late, at around 5pm. As if he had some premonition of what was about to happen, Fin decided he would not come with us up to the roof area and instead stay in the street, taking up a position sitting on the pavement opposite number 3. There were only a few groupies hanging around this time as John and I went into the Max Factor building, up the stairs and presently emerged out of their roof top exit and into the vast Mary Poppinsesque landscape of brick, gabled and flat roofs and huge red brick chimneys. This time, comfortable and confident on our second mission, we stood for a while to take in the vista, amazed at the scene we'd paid little attention to on our first visit.

We sauntered around, exploring the areas further afield from where the Beatles had played. I left John to it and, walking to the edge of the rooftop overlooking 3 Savile Row, I shouted and waved down at Fin. He acknowledged, just as John came running over to me in blind panic. *"They've closed the bloody Max Factor exit and the Apple one's shut too!"*

Bugger. It was well after 5pm now. We weren't going to get into the studios today, or so we thought, and as John disappeared amongst the array of chimneys to look for another entry point into another building so that we could get back down to the street, I called down to Fin *"We're stuck up here. They've closed the exits!"*

Fin cupped his hands to his ears and I realised he couldn't make out what I was saying. Looking around, I spotted an old beaten up biro, which I picked up and managed to scribble on a tiny piece of scruffy paper I found in my pocket *"Stuck. Can't get down. Go sleep in the van if we're not there in 30 mins. Come back tomorrow morning"*.

However, I had the van key. As I was walking around looking for another larger piece of paper so that I could wrap the message and the car key together and throw it down to Fin, I heard some police sirens in the distance; not an unusual sound in central London. Looking again over the edge, a Triumph 2000 police car sped up Savile Row, blue lights flashing, and stopped outside the building, decanting what must have been half a dozen rozzers into number 3. Bloody hell, I thought. Someone has beaten us to it and broken in.

Continuing to peer down at the street below, more police cars arrived decanting more rozzers. I was thinking that this must be very serious. Bugger me. It's an IRA Bomb attack, and we're right on top of it!! I swung around to shout a warning to John when my attention was drawn to the Apple Studio rooftop exit as it burst open, and like a scene from a Keystone Cops silent movie, out spilled a ream of rozzers tripping clumsily one on top of the other. The penny dropped. Maybe I should have, like Churchill, studied history, thus perhaps avoiding a repetition of the police infested event of January 30, 1969. But my fate became clear. I stood, stunned, as the Keystone Cops un-tangled themselves and rushed toward their quarry. Me.

Forget the pussycats of 'Minder', The Professionals' and 'Life on Mars'. This lot were *really* viscous twats. All five of them managed to grab me and roughly push me toward the edge of the roof, one of them threatening *"..Easy to accidentally fall off the edge, sunbeam?"* while another one bawled *"You're nicked ma' son. What are you doing up here then? Waiting to do a breaking and entry job, eh? eh?"*

I still had in my grasp the note I'd written to Fin, and like a naïve imbecile, presented it as evidence, explaining, rather disingenuously I suppose, that we were innocents, stranded after coming up to see this famous spot, and that we were trying to find a route back down. As it was grabbed from my hand, roughly crumpled and jettisoned over the edge without a glance, I realised the word 'innocent' didn't seem to figure in these buggers' vocabulary.

"Go and find the other f**king northern twat" bad cop shouted to the re-enforcements who had just arrived, stumbling out of the Apple Corps Studio exit. Wow, we must have either been very dangerous criminals to merit this level of attention, or the rozzers at the nearby station were bored out of their thick empty heads. I'd say it was the latter.

"Where is he? We know there're two of you"

"I don't know. He went to look for a way..."

"Shut the f**k up" confirmed that he wasn't interested in anything that might get in the way of promotion after arresting two dangerous hippie terrorists with a non-London and therefore confusing accent, brandishing a little piece of paper and a knackered old writing weapon on the rooftops of central London.

After another few minutes of verbal and physical abuse, bad cop spotted the other rozzers slouching like gorillas as they dejectedly returned from their search.

"Where is he?" bad cop closely reiterated to my face with his IPA beer breath.

"There...he's behind you" was my pantomime reply.

John, hiding only a few yards away from the best crack-police-rooftop-search-team in London, had started to slowly sidle out from behind a chimneystack, shouting *"I give up..."*, both hands in the air like a dangerous armed criminal. The five slouching rozzers leapt into life, slamming chaotically into each other as they lunged toward him and manhandled this dangerous threat to London's citizens over to where I stood.

"What are you f**king doing up here, Butch f**king Cassidy? Waiting to do a breaking and entry job?" was this time directed at John, who confirmed my story, but which only had a more maddening influence on the

twat, which resulted in us both being dragged along behind the Apple Corps Studios exit area. We found ourselves pushed to the limit of a ledge which overlooked, some twenty feet below, a glass atrium, through which could be seen a white marble floor another three floors down.

"See that down there sunbeam? Nasty do, if you accidentally slipped while resisting arrest, eh?".

John and I glanced at each other, realising we couldn't get away with cheeking this lot, and so in acquiescence, we tried to look humble, guilty, and pliant. Difficult.

"Get these northern twats back to the station".

As we were led down through the Apple Corps building and bundled into one of the three blue-light-flashing Triumph 2000s, much to the safely detached amusement of Fin watching it all from amongst a small crowd that had gathered on the opposite pavement, I had visions of the impact of this event on ITN's evening news; BONG...: "Two dangerous northerners arrested on Savile Row rooftops!" BONG...: "Russia declares war on America". I looked around, winking at Fin, but unfortunately couldn't see any news teams.

While an only insipidly interested audience of passers-by looked on, their ultimate destination probably being even less interesting than the event they were watching, the police car sped off on its embarrassingly short journey to Savile Row station, bells ringing and blue lights flashing to effect some drama into this highly insignificant arrest. On our arrival, it all transpired to be déjà vu with a London accent. We were split up and each interrogated in a yellowing smoky room with a single brown nicotine stained light bulb. Of course our stories tallied, and feeling we were now relatively safe amongst some normal looking admin. rozzers, and were, more importantly, at ground level, the little insolence fellow stirred within me.

Tiring of our intransigence and our fairly believable account of events, although we didn't mention the other visit and the nicked song sheets, we were bought together again and interviewed by not-so-bad cop.

"You do realise that you could end up being kept here in a cell until we get to the bottom of this?"

"Is there any chance of transferring us to the police station where we live then, so we don't miss Titch's party?", the little insolent fellow within me responded, much to John's amusement.

Thankfully, not-so-bad cop just rolled his eyes and left the room.

Good cop presently entered and announced *"Right you time wasting little buggers, get out of here, and get out of London. If you come to our attention ANYWHERE in London tonight, you'll both be in deep trouble".*

A completely empty, unenforceable and, I foolishly thought, irrelevant threat, but we were glad to be free as we made our way back to 3 Savile Row to find

Fin still there, eager to hear the full story, and laughing like a drain at the comment about Titch's party. It turned out that it wasn't an IRA bomb attack that attracted the rozzers onto the Apple Corps rooftop, but, as Fin found out, it was a caretaker who'd spotted us from an Atrium area below.

It was almost midnight when we got back to Highgate and the van, and although the party loomed the following evening, I was too tired to drive back, and so we agreed to have a few hours sleep on the feather mattress in the back of the van, parking in a side street.

Dreaming about parachuting from a rooftop, clutching Beatles song sheets as police fired at me with water pistols, I was firstly awoken by John, announcing that he was 'a bit hungry and couldn't sleep and wanted to go for a walk, so would I unlock the doors and let him out'.

I was secondly awoken by John a short time after he'd disappeared into the gloom of a Highgate night, when he knocked on the van rear window, demanding to be quickly let in. As he leaned to crawl into the van, fifteen pounds of strange green fruit rolled out of an improvised sack fashioned from his jumper, onto the mattress, awaking a very pissed-off Fin.

Before I had time to ask, John reported proudly *"I pushed on the door of this shop I was passing and it just opened and there was nobody in there so I helped myself."*. I looked down at the avocado pears. Why bloody avocado pears?

"For Christ's sake, this really is f**king breaking and entry. The rozzers will make this charge stick, nicking a ton of bloody Avocado Pears from a shop, unlocked or otherwise. We'll have to get out of here. Now!"

Titch's party was a good one, with plenty of drink, laughter, bragging and the very welcome and wholly expected notoriety, of course. We'd spent most of the previous night on the car park at Watford Gap services re-telling and therefore re-living our latest adventure in preparation for the party, and drinking shite coffee while we struggled to de-stone bucketfuls of bloody avocados.

This extract from 'Ask Ron & Eddie' by E Langley De Montfort is © Lawrence Milner 2015, Decade Books UK

United Brown States of America Road Trip

by Edward Dixon Elliott

No relation to the famous Jerimiah Dixon who surveyed the USA and Canada and plotted the Mason-Dixon line. This family were a combination of entrepreneurs who carried out construction work, believed in education and constructed many major construction projects. The name gives away the recalcitrant nature of the family. Border reivers are Elliott and Dixon. An Elliott or a Dixon on their own is bad enough, but an amalgam of Elliotts and Dixons is truly too much for most peoples' sensibilities. Unruly drinking, womanising, sheep stealing and fighting men. I'm surprised they are allowed to travel anywhere given their nature. However, I suppose America let in the mafia which has been absorbed into society, and it grew the Ku Klux Klan, so we're not really that bad after all?

Visa granted!

Brown.

Brown is the colour of American hotels.

Brown carpets, brown paintwork, brown tiles and cream everywhere else.

Try finding a dark framed pair of glasses in a brown room. It requires a lot of luck. I know this for a fact.

The adventure begins with the brown road trip today from Dallas.

Going South

Hotels should have a brown star rating. We are in the Lone Star State with one star for White Anglo Saxon Protestants (WASPS). The Crowne Plaza in has a 3 star brown rating, let's see what transpires with the rest of the journey? The manager of the hotel greeted me with "How are you?". I said good, but told a lie as my arse isn't. However, that has a life if its own. Are you from the UK he said. Durham was the reply and he then proceeded to tell me how much his first wife loved to go to the Metro centre at Newcastle. Small world eh! That was his first wife.

As Mike Frost used to say, "With divorce everything is split equally. The wife gets the house, the man gets the mortgage, the wife gets the kids, the husband gets to maintenance, etc." I think you see where we are going on this one. It brightened my morning to find someone who loved the Lake District and was generally cheerful.

Well goodbye Dallas, we really should have another day here, it has loads to see and I like it. However, it is not Stetsons and cowboy boots; never saw one of them!

Predominantly black and poor where we were, the tourists are white and well heeled.

More cheap fuel to buy

We've arrived at Little Rock and we have another brown hotel, this one is just a two star brown, but brown nonetheless.

The waiter described the local ales and he recommended a brown ale called 'Brown Dog'. I told him the story of Newcastle Brown ale also known as dog due to the ruse of telling your wife, "I'm going to take the dog for a walk" thus allowing the man of the house with dog to frequent a local pub and imbibe some Newcastle Brown ale. He then reposted with his tale of the naming of his local brew called Brown Dog.

We were in Little Rock, home of Bill Clinton, but north of the river was North Little Rock. Are you with me up to now?

Good.

The locals used to take their unwanted brown dogs north of the river and leave them there. Thus alleviating themselves of the burden of man's best friend. When that cowboy wrote the song 'My Four Legged Friend", was it a horse or a dog? My wonderful one two three four legged friend.

Touché .

The trip to Memphis was fairly un-eventful. Memphis isn't brown, although the rivers are. I thought I could finish with the brown theme. I reserve the right to return to it if required.

Memphis.

I'm sitting here drinking my Newcastle Brown ale whilst the lightening storm goes on over the Mississippi. Air to air lightening occurs at about every second. It is a pure daylight when it happens. The rain has gone and it is much cooler now. It has been a long day.

Reflecting on Memphis, it is a stark contrast of life styles. White trailer trash diners and sophisticated restaurants. I could not cope with the noise, grease and lousy music. So much for Ashley and southern sophistication.

On Monday nights they have a special $20 three course meal; the chef likes to try new recipes (though I suspect it is his night off and the trainees are in).

Don't really care as we get to dine in a nice setting with a tablecloth and proper service. Gladys was our waitress and she must have been 60 with painted-on eyebrows in a permanently surprised fashion. I liked her eyebrows, they made me feel at home.

On a table next to us were five old ladies who dominated the room because everyone could hear their mundane conversation. Obviously there for the $20 special, they drank the water only and split the bill, which took some time. It was straight from 'Gone With the Wind'. Along with the old colonel and family with jacket, tie and much decorum. However listening to them was brilliant as they were all like Miss Daisy and talked in that 'never you mind' way that you think is only in the movies.

Gladys, who would not have been out of place in a hamburger, joint took our order, returning with a breadbasket with something sprinkled with icing sugar which did not resemble bread buns, and a plate of pink stuff that resembled taramasalata. When questioned, she said "They was popovers with strawberry butter, you know, redneck Yorkshire pudding"!

The Yorkshire pud was lovely but I backed away from the strawberry butter.

We had a bottle of wine, which flummoxed Gladys because she flapped around finding an ice bucket, then kept flapping around every time we took a sip to top up the glass. She kept saying, "Y'all can take the wine back to your room if you don't finish it, and put it in the fridge. Y'all know where your fridge is in your room? It is in your TV cabinet." It must be unusual in these parts to drink a whole bottle of wine.

We finished it no problem. The wine cost more than the meal.

When I think of it, the guy in Dallas said, "A whole bottle?"

I've spent the day at Gracelands which was an essential must-do. I wasn't disappointed. The private jet planes were amazing. Almost like a 60s film set for James Bond, but real. The King's gold records were everywhere and the organisation was pretty slick.

It could not happen in the UK?

Sun records was also a must-do. It was amazing in that the sound engineers had recorded conversations between the performers such as Elvis, Cash, Jerry Lee Lewis etc. It brought the tour to life. Met a lad from Eire whom I had a long chat to; travel creates events like these. Memorable events!!! He was doing the tourist stuff as well. We both made no excuse for our sheep-like following of the tourists. Leaving Sun records, I found St Blues guitar shop where a man was making the most beautiful handmade guitars. I was offered a chance to play one but refused due to lack of talent. I bought two packs of guitar strings to take home. I really wanted to give it a go but he must have to listen to some real dross. I couldn't inflict it on him.

Sun records (A failed musician wondering what might be?)

The civil rights museum was attached to the Loretta hotel where Martin Luther King was assassinated. Guess what? It was by a rifle from a window again. You would think someone would put a stop to gun ownership? You would think you had been there before because the film footage made it so familiar. Below is a photograph of a woman who you wouldn't win an argument with. She has been living on the pavement, or sidewalk as we are in America, for over 26 years, as a protest to the money spent on the Martin Luther King museum.

Outside the Loretta Hotel

Strange they will shoot people around here, but they won't kill a duck and therefore it is off the menu at the Peabody hotel. The ducks do a walk, orchestrated by the duck master in a red jacket, from the hotel fountain to the elevator where they continue their journey back to their home on the roof of the hotel. There must have been 200 people watching the mallard ducks. The only daffy ducks around were the audience. Although I would say I saw a Goofy, and was that Elmer Fudd on the balcony with his gun?

Lobster is on the menu tonight, so it will have to be accompanied by a whole bottle of wine. I find their view of alcohol odd. You can get hammered on spirits, cocktails or beer. But a whole bottle of wine? Well I never - miss Daisy!!! My mint julep is all a body needs. I think not!

It's July 4 and the city is preparing for fireworks tonight in the land of the free. Except they tip everyone. It isn't free. The man on immigration asked me, will I be doing anything special for July 4? I replied that I'm making a statement and drinking tea on independence day. That's the best a man can do! He smiled and got the irony straight away, which is unusual in the States!

Waiting is a major part of marriage, when the couple are together. When not together; waiting is taken out of the daily schedule, thus freeing up time for your own interests and activities.

For the future, waiting will take up a significant part of the day.

More waiting has been found as I'm now in a shopping mall the size of Cumbria. Aptly called North Park. GPS navigation system is mandatory to find your way around this. Big isn't in it. Even the Parks are huge in Texas. Everything is bigger and better. There is so much space. I have a dislike of the mobile telephones intrusion into my life. However in this case I can wander aimlessly around, with a text available to reconnect me to the shopping expedition, after studying the locals of all shapes and sizes.

The beautiful are very beautiful, young, firm and generally gorgeous from a male perspective. The not so gorgeous are just that, fat with appetites the size of a starving lion. The feeding times at the mall are continuous and the public can observe this without restriction. The lion handlers are called Big Mac, Panda Express the Chinese keeper, Hibachi San, the Japanese keeper, Burgher King (he must be Austrian) and Wimpy the Irish handler who has a construction company in the UK. A truly international group of animal handlers. The only handler who I could see that was not taking part was Happy Salad; I presume a man of cheerful demeanour which the lions dislike.

Food is soaked in flavourings to disguise the taste of whatever the poor animal was at the outset. Our medieval ancestors would have been proud that food taste could be disguised in such a way that any rotting flesh could be devoured with impunity. The downside is diabetes and heart disease. The drug industry must love these eating habits.

Long live consumerism.

A band has just started up inside this mausoleum to not living. I must go and investigate? The longer I sit, the more the consumers look like something from an Aldous Huxley novel, marching without thinking, texting without any awareness of the surrounding clones. If there is a bottleneck, the cry from the uniformed controllers is to form a line. Americans are very good at forming lines. So much so they resemble Russians in the bread queue. There's a disturbing thought!!! The land of the free acting like Ruskies. The Russians embracing consumerism! It's a strange old shopping mall. I'm always at my worst when bored. I could do anything. Well not quite. The lion feeders won't get me. But a nice bottle of chilled Sierra Nevada pale ale might if I wasn't driving.

Enough observation for the moment. Time to find a nice coffee shop with sophisticated ambiance. The coffee shop holds 1000 people and therefore not intimate enough for my needs.

There is a God in heaven. I've just found an open courtyard in the middle of the mall that is silent. I have purchased a very large tub of lemon sorbet with M & Ms mixed in. Still people-watching but now in the sun at 94°F with sugar level at a max. Life isn't all that bad, except for the diabetes with all of that sugar.

Time for a bottle of wine?

Why is it when you are desperate for a drink you can never find the bottle opener or cork screw?

The One that Got Away
Fishing in Montana
by Terry McCleary , Tonica, USA

In July of 2002, our family made the trek west. We stopped at many of the normal sites, such as Wall Drug, the Bad Lands and Mount Rushmore in South Dakota. In Wyoming, we went to the Cheyenne Rodeo Days, Devil's Tower, and ultimately Yellowstone National Park. But one of my most memorable parts of the trip was our time in Montana.

We started our trip on a Friday and arrived on Monday in Dillon, Montana, where a friend of ours, Mike, was there waiting on us. We immediately hit the water. Because we only had enough time for one river in the daytime left, we went just a short drive south of town to the Poindexter Slough.

Mike and I caught many fish that week, but the one this story is about is the one that got away. We all have pictures of big fish in our photo albums, on our phones and computers, but the fish that my son and I will never forget was never netted, beached, snagged or otherwise caught.

Thursday evening after dinner, Mike and I were going to go back out fishing, but his back was giving him some trouble so he stayed back at the hotel. I looked at Alec, my son, and asked if he would want to go. He jumped at the chance. The Poindexter Slough was close, but a little deeper than what I thought he would want to wade so we opted to go to the section of the Beaverhead River at the southern end of town. Mike had some luck here earlier in the week and it had good access for an 8 year old fly fisherman.

By this time in Alec's life he has caught many Blue Gill from the farm pond back home in Illinois and a few Trout from the spring creeks of Southwest Wisconsin. So his casting was good. All I needed to do was pick the fly and help guide him to where the fish were hiding. As I had said, Mike and I had some good fortune here earlier in the week, so I was confident I could get him into some pan sized Trout near the bottom of the weir in the river. There was some impressive eddies here that constantly churns up the food flowing in the river.

This was Alec's time to fish and my time to take some pictures of the beautiful scenery and of him casting and hopefully catching a fish or two. I was telling him where to cast the fly, but because he was left handed and the spot was set up perfectly for a right handed approach he had some issues getting the fly to the mark. We were standing on an island in the river and casting across to the north bank where a multiflora rose bush was overhanging the water. This was one spot I wanted to hit while I was here earlier, but never got the chance. Alec handed me his fly rod and I showed him the spot I wanted him to hit. The first cast, I missed the mark. The second cast was closer so I tried one more time. What happened next I could not have ever imagined. The third cast I dropped the fly in the hole and the line went taut. At that point the hook was not set. The fly we tied on was called a Yellow Sally on a number 16 hook.

I handed the rod to Alec and said, "Bring him in". He said, "Bring what in". At the same time he saw the line move and he set the hook like a master fisherman. At this point the race was on. The fish went downstream, upstream and finally broke the surface of the water. I am not sure whose eyes were bigger, Alec's or mine. I knew the fish was big but WOW! When he broke the water surface, we then knew the fish was big and he was brown. He was so big that the most he could muster

Some Other People's Lives

after he made it through the surface was to fall ever so gracefully on his side back into the water.

Alec continued to fight him, reeling in line when he came towards him and let line out when he wanted to run. It dawned on me I had better get some pictures of the battle. Unfortunately, I was shaking so bad because of the excitement that they were all blurred. At this point I remembered that I didn't have any of my gear, no rod, no reel, no vest and unfortunately no net. The 'Ole boy' was getting tired and was beginning to slow down. Alec was able to reel him in to about 10 ft. away, but he made one last run downstream. I asked Alec to try to beach him on the south bank where we entered the river not remembering how fast the water flowed on that side of the island. Alec made his move toward the bank where I was carefully keeping the rod tip up and tension on the line. Amazingly enough the brown followed until he hit the faster water and made a fierce lunge downstream and got away. I was in tears while Alec at the ripe old age of 8 said "Dad, we'll get another one". I was so impressed at his calmness, while I could hardly stand.

We sat on the bank thinking how we could have done this any differently. I grabbed the end of the line thinking the line had broken but to my surprise I saw the fly at the end. I looked at the fly a little closer and saw that the hook had bent to the side, giving him the chance to escape capture.

Well, at this point my nerves were shot. I thought we should commemorate the event somehow so I took Alec by the fly shop, Frontier Anglers, there in

Dillon. When I walked in I had in my head that I would like to get Alec a nice pin to put on his vest. I didn't see any right off, but asked the gentlemen behind the counter if they had any. He said sure. I found a nice one with a trout and the state name Montana on it, but I was shocked at the price and said so to the gentlemen. He asked why I wanted the pin so I told him the story. He came around the counter and took a look at Alec and asked where we caught up with the big brown, on the far side of the river? We said yes. Up by the weir? We said yes. Over by the bush overhanging the cut bank? We said yes again. He proclaimed that they had caught the same fish last fall and measured him then to be over 29 inches long.

The gentlemen asked to see the fly that Alec used, so he reluctantly handed it over to him. The gentleman immediately saw that the hook was bent and proclaimed that the hook shouldn't have bent that way and told Alec if I bought the pin he would throw in a hat to put in on for nothing. What could I do but buy the pin?

Alec grew a foot taller in that shop while the gentleman told that story to another man in the shop. Now I know that there are other fish in that river. That there is only a small chance that the fish we caught was the fish that clerk was talking about, but that is exactly what we chose to believe. While the details of the trip get fuzzier with time, I will not forget that evening with my son.

Spiritual Experiences
by Edward Dixon Elliott

This didn't start in St Mary Magdalene church as a choir boy. My family are scattered around the grounds, so maybe it should if you believe in a spirit World. I like the Red Indian concept of a spirit world and us being part of it, this was maybe because my father showed a great deal of interest in Indian spirituality? Who knows? He had too much time alone on an aircraft carrier in the Pacific.

My sister and I shared a childhood bedroom. She awoke in terror one night when she saw me turn into my grandfather Elliott and his face floated off through the ceiling. Imagination? I would say so, but this was very real to my sister. The mind is a little understood beast and it can be a beast if left uncontrolled.

I would have to wait a long time until Buddhist meditation saw me view the world around me in a very different way.

With the Buddhism came a change of friends. Some of which I still keep in contact with today. Their view of the World is very much an amazing journey when links are made to events that look like, THERE IS A PLAN! Is there a plan? I have no idea? I feel I'm a little too entrenched in the real World to be part of a spiritual one, yet I feel I am the loser for not having the belief in the amazing and unfathomable events called life.

I believe a world without magic and mystery is a pretty poor one and I speak with my RILEM senior scientist hat on here. There is no conflict between dealing with facts and imagination. I just have to find a way to make the imagination into measurable facts. I suppose that's why I love my research so much. I am wandering. Back to matters spiritual.

The strangest event I had after meditating was to walk along the street at street light level whilst I looked down at myself at street level. Weird and God only knows how that works? I can't really say that because I can't rely on God to explain that to me if you are to believe the last paragraph? As a passing acquaintance once said to me, whilst we were drunk on his boat in Paxos, we just haven't found the science to explain this yet. Science or not it was one hell of an afternoon, whilst I played House of the Rising Sun on his Gibson guitar and we all howled the words like red neck "ye ha"s. Memories are made of this. "Sweet sweet the memories you made for me". Smile!

The reason I attended a spiritualist church is long and convoluted. It concerned lots of alcohol, false bravado (or fear), and a great deal of scepticism.

Once the alcohol had worn off I came to my senses and fear of the unknown replaced the false bravado. I didn't want to go but upon being accused of cowardice I had to. It's a man ego thing! I think the inverse law applies. Big ego, small, well I think you know!

All I could think of was no messages for me. If you can hear me, no messages! If it was nonsense why was I so unsettled?

So the church service began with a Christian hymn. Phew, that was a relief. No sacrificial goat (the Welsh community centres were using all of these.) Phase one over, and I was feeling a little more confident. Then this chap stood up and tried to connect with those who had "passed over" (that's dead people in simple language). All I could think of was, "not me". So this man said to the girl in front of me, "Do you know anyone passed over who worked in the building industry?" She said no, I said yes, but this was directed at the young lady in front of me. Ok he said, this man is agitated for not communicating with him. "Have you any relatives in farming?" No she said. I said yes, but this was directed at the young lady in front of me. Ok he said, this man is agitated for not communicating with him again. He is saying it's that long haired young lady. My father called me a young lady due to my long hair. 'Long' being a concept derived from the military years and national service. I wondered, builder, farming relatives and long hair as a private joke. I said nothing. Bugger me, if I wanted a message I'd have sent a letter by post.

The medium said the man on the other side was becoming very agitated. Out of absolute exasperation he said, "I have a message for you, young lady."

It was very specific and went like this.

"All of my time at my last address I had wanted to carry out a repair to my chimney stack. I couldn't due to the state of the neighbour's roof. The time was now right to carry out this repair".

My sister lived in the old family home and she still does to this day.

I left the spiritualist church confident that it was a load of mumbo jumbo.

The next morning whilst walking to the office, I met my sister who lives in my old family home. She was aghast and covered in soot. She told me that her chimney stack had collapsed overnight. In addition she told me the neighbour had just moved out so that access from their roof was possible for the first time during the occupation of the family house.

Oh dear! My interpretation of the whole thing was floundering, lost for any sensible logic, I just repaired the stack. In retrospect, I should have put an insurance claim in. I was bamboozled.

Well that was the end of all things spiritual? Not really. There were a couple of very odd and linked events that started with Irmgard, a friend's mother, dying of cancer. I'd been to see Irmgard and she mentioned she would love to see her son and his friends reunited. The friends were, me, Pete (her son) and Geoff who was mainly Pete's good friend. My only hope was to locate our common friend's father, to re-establish some form of contact, as Geoff had left for Diplo (Pakistan) as a seismologist. Geoff's father ended his working life as a caretaker with Sunderland council. It was a slim chance of success.

As I left Irmgard's house the left turn turned into a right turn.......The destination was unknown. But when

I stopped in the middle of a field I met a man who looked after the caretakers for Sunderland council. Hang on there. This is nonsense !

We exchanged telephone numbers and he telephoned me with the depressing news that Geoff's father had died, but that he had his son's telephone number if that was of any use?

That's how I was reacquainted with an old mate in common. He was lost for 20 years and I found him in 20 minutes. Illogical mumbo jumbo. Somebody please tell me how this is possible?

I'll leave the tale at this point because there were more strange events of equal difficulty to make logical sense of. For instance, when a mate's house wouldn't sell, I said you're not cursing the man who sold you the house are you? There was good reason to feel bitter as the house had been renovated by cowboy builders and was going to be difficult to sell. Then there was a ringing in our ears and I asked my mates to find him and say sorry and the house would sell. Where do I get these wild statements from? They couldn't locate him so I took a guess and said to try the local spiritualist church and speak to him. It could have been "try Buckingham Palace" for all I knew. I was a complete stranger to the area and had never met the man.

The rest is history; he was where I said he would be, he did feel abused by the torrent of hate, and saying sorry worked as the house sold one week later.

Ok, nonsense I hear you say. I can't really blame you! I wrote it, but I wouldn't believe it!

A Visit to a Star

by E Langley De Montfort

As John and I gazed skyward, the sound of Sibelius' 'At the Castle Gate' could be heard through his Mum's council house window, announcing the start of 'The Sky at Night'. We watched it and agreed that an adventure was in order, in the form of a completely impromptu and unannounced visit to Patrick Moore's house at the other end of the country. We thought he looked a nice accommodating chap on the telly.

The Four, me, John, Fin and Neil, along with two slip streamers, Liam and Patch S, threw our sleeping bags and a bright orange, seen-better-days un - waterproofed Blacks ridge tent into the back of the van and drove south out of the city heading for Selsey Bill, over 330 miles away.

Patch S worked hard in long shifts and so we had to wait until 6 pm to pick him up the following Friday evening. A long dark haired hippie and a beautiful person, he was often chatted up in the smoke and gloom of the disco dance floors. He was as heterosexually 'straight' as one could be, so much so, I think, that he wasn't bothered, and I think was even flattered, that he got such attention from anyone.

Patch S got his name from black leather knee patches on the Silver Spur jeans he always wore. He looked poverty-stricken and underprivileged, but as a consequence of working long hours, he earned lots of money.

I was present when he bought his only indulgent luxury item; an Omega watch valued at £350.00. The snooty high-class jeweller's sales assistance looked him up and down before he reluctantly and guardedly allowed him to examine the top of the range timepiece. He nearly swallowed his teeth when Patch S asked if he could take it outside to more *'meaningfully appreciate its beauty'*, and it was only after Patch S produced a wad of fivers from his scruffy jeans pocket that his demeanour changed.

"Would sir like the watch gift wrapped?" was the pre-emptive and erroneous response, the assistant still of the opinion that such an unrefined looking youngster couldn't possibly even contemplate owning such a treasure.

It was a long but typically jolly drive that night. I was the only one who could legally drive the company van due to insurance limitations, which I ignored anyway by consistently filling the back of the van with fellow adventurers.

We so loved these events, always unsure as to how they would turn out, but always rewarded on our return with an entertaining tale or two with which to impress the attentive listeners; mostly Jake, Rod and particularly our schoolgirl, friends who joined us most weekend evenings on our return.

We stopped off for a break at some services on the M1, where Liam bought a 'Rustler' magazine, producing, as only he could, much hilarity from the nude pictures and readers letters as we drove toward the 'big smoke', as smoggy London was often referred to at the time. The comment *"Bloody hell. I've been out with her. She lives down my street!"* had John and Neil, who lived near Liam, fighting to get a look at this large breasted trollop, just in case they could claim the slightest bit of kudos in having seen her on the street.

There being no M25 at that time, we presently made our way through the centre of London, quite silently, each of us beginning to feel pretty tired. We were staring out of the van, mesmerised by the unfamiliar architecture, the busy streets full of people at such a late hour, and the dazzling lights of the west end. London is one of those places where you can walk in the midst of so many and yet be so alone; so accomplished and yet so desolate.

Wander through London's crowded streets and you walk amongst the has-beens (e.g. Alvin Stardust), the wannabes (e.g. me) and the successful 'beings' (e.g. Bill Nighy, Richard Curtis and Alan Yentob). I wonder if *they,* the significant amongst humankind, also think much about just how insignificant, how transitory and ultimately pointless *all* of us really are?

All born. All live. All love. All die.

All exist for only the briefest of moments in a vast, endless universe.

Maybe that is all there is.

We had, as usual, set out with no bloody idea where we could sleep at three in the morning, and it was quite the exception that we even took a tent as we mostly slept on the feather mattress in the back of the van. This exception occurred because we saw the weather forecast which predicted showers in the south.

The consensus, as the rain showers started to mess with the view through the mucky windscreen, was that we needed to find some lay-by or forest track so some of us could pitch the tent under cover, providing some protection for the leaky tent, while the rest of us laid up nearby in the van. We found such a place near Chichester, but as we searched in the glare of the headlights for a place on the forest floor where we could pitch the tent, bones were discovered. They were only bones of badgers or foxes or the likes, but three brave, fearless derring-doers of the party freaked out and refused to sleep anywhere near that spot, questioning why such a mix of animal bones might be there. Devil worship and sacrifice? Admittedly, the whole area had a spooky and supernatural ambience, and I was pleased to give up in the end and drive on, awakened and refreshed by the search and the break in the journey, arriving in the streets of Selsey as the morning sun began to illustrate its presence as a translucent white layer on the frost covered ramshackle terracotta roof of an ex-cricketer's mansion, burned down and left to rot some years before. The ideal spot to fetch up I thought, its ground floor interior providing some shelter and concealment for the tent, the weed ridden untendered drive providing off-street parking for the van in which Patch S and Liam decided to sleep.

It was bloody freezing when I awoke only a few restless hours later to the full glare of a winter's morning sun. It was streaming in through the smoke blackened holes that one could have once described as 'windows', illuminating our orange tent like a coastal beacon. A beacon that any passing rozzer could easily spot through the gaping hole in the wall, a hole which we failed to notice in our haste to pitch the tent and get a few hours kip. Sliding stiffly out of my sleeping bag as I aroused the rest of this freezing madcap party of indoor camping voyagers, I went out to hammer on the frost-encrusted door of the van. As they came lumbering out looking like extras in a scene from 'Shaun of the Dead', a man in a snug overcoat and furry Russian hat nodded a bemused and muted half greeting as he passed by, newspaper under arm, furtively glancing back from a safe distance as he quickened his pace. I guessed it wouldn't be long before the rozzers arrived. Apparently they did, according to a man in a pub who engaged us in conversation early that afternoon. But as ever with the rozzers, they just never quite get it right. Our source informed us that they had taken a quick tour of the area, and presumed that the geezer in the furry hat was mistaken, there being no 'bright orange tent full of mad hippies camped in a burnt out house'. Our source had an FM radio tuned to the police frequencies.

We had moved the van to a side street and parked it under cover of a bloody big Luton van, splitting up so as not to attract too much attention, each spending the morning walking the shingle beach and exploring the village, having agreed to meet in the pub for a much needed warm-up lunch. It turned out that our FM snooping man-in-the-pub friend was from our city. Unbelievable. But then we'd often meet people from our city who'd settled in various parts of the UK.

We told him of some of our adventures, and that we'd driven through the night from his 'old town' to see our 'astronomic' hero. He listened with great interest and evident pleasure, asking us to elaborate on some of our other derring-dos we happened to mention. I had a fancy he'd been a bit of a lad himself at one time, perhaps 'emigrating' to a place as far south as it was possible to go to avoid the consequences. He didn't, however, ask us to keep his location secret, and after talking at length about 'the old town' and the good old days before cars choked the streets of the council estates and stopped us kids playing 'skippy' and other wholesome games, we left him smiling and looking thoughtful with his pint in one hand and waving a burned-down-fag-farewell with the other. I'd like to think he enjoyed that brief encounter, and that we'd left him a happier man for it.

It was I who was charged with the task of knocking on Patrick Moore's door that afternoon. The others huddled together around the gate, heads hung down like naughty schoolboys who had been, or were about to be, getting up to no good.

Walking along the short garden path that lead to the glazed porch, I gazed with envy at the beautiful house with its thatched roof, so far removed geographically and, most poignantly, aesthetically, from my working class hovel back home. As I waited for a response from me knocking timidly on the door, faltering a little as I mused on me having any right whatsoever to be there, I looked about me at the vast garden which hosted his now famous reflector telescopes, and at his rickety old bicycle which leaned against the wall next to the porch, and on which he famously rode around the village.

It seemed an age before I started to turn toward the gate, thinking, foolishly really, as I understood his aging mother never went out, that there was no-one at home, when I glimpsed through the glass door the advancing larger-than-life frame of Patrick Moore walking toward me with a spritely spring in his step and a jolly smiling monocled face. As he opened the door I hesitantly turned back to face him and said, having not even thought of what I should say if we met, "*Errr, could I have your autograph please?*"

What a bloody stupid thing to say, but he laughed and beckoned me to come in. Gesturing toward the gate, I told him there were 'a few more of us', whereupon he popped his head around the door and cheerfully ordered the gang to follow us into his house.

Not in any of our considered expectations did we anticipate ending up chatting to Patrick Moore, sitting in his study and drinking Guinness from his collection of tankards while we discussed telescopes, the rings of Saturn and the American space programme. He was such a gentleman; no hard edge to him at all, and possessing that rare attribute of being able to actually converse with you rather than talk at you, genuinely interested as he was in all we had to say. Of course we didn't tell him about our shady derring-dos and adventures. It wasn't the sort of subject that would naturally be raised in astronomy discussions, was it, and I think we all felt we didn't want to compromise the warmth and friendship he'd shown us by revealing what a set of uneducated northern chancers we really were. However, when he asked when and how we had arrived in Selsey, we did admit to 'driving all night and sleeping in a tent in an old burnt out house down the road because we'd taken fright at the discovery of animal bones in a forest'. He found this highly amusing, seeming to genuinely think it was a jolly jape, and proceeded to tell us that the house had belonged to a cricketer before a fire tore through it some years back. He said, with a sigh of resignation, that it had remained in that state for far too long. I was rather glad of it.

Some Other People's Lives

While Patrick went off to fetch some tea and biscuits, John and I, with his permission, took out the Instamatic camera and snapped a few pictures of us in his large and very academic looking study, Patrick posing with us upon his return. En route to the garden, he took us through the house to meet his mother, a quiet and charming woman with a warm smile. She indulged us in a few pleasantries, and I wondered, her giving nothing away in this regard, whether what seemed to me a premature curtailment of our conversation with her was due to the repetitive nature of this sort of occurrence, Patrick often entertaining many groups of visitors and dignitaries, or whether, and I'm unsure which version I prefer, she sensed that we actually were a set of northern chancers, albeit chancers who were pleasant enough and interested in her son and his passion for astronomy.

After a tour around the telescopes during which we talked basic astronomy and took more pictures, I reluctantly suggested that we should leave, acknowledging his very great kindness in entertaining and welcoming us unannounced hippie strangers into his house. I felt so very privileged, a feeling I was hardly familiar with, when he insistently invited us back that evening to do some stargazing.

As Zeus would have it, attracting his attention as we travelled half way across the UK to look through the world's most famous astronomer's telescopes, the bloody sky clouded over that evening and the best we could do was to thank Patrick profusely as we marvelled again at his generosity, his house and his telescopes, posing once more for more evidential photographs of 'Patrick and Us', to be presented in the pub back home as proof to the less adventurous friends with their interested and interesting girlfriends that we'd done it again. I was getting quite fond of this stuff. So fond that we did the Patrick Moore trip again one cloudy non-stargazing night six months later. Zeus found out about that trip, too.

This extract from 'Ask Ron & Eddie' by E Langley De Montfort is © Lawrence Milner 2015, Decade Books UK

Alan's Angling Adventures
by Alan Richardson

Where to start? (With an alliteration I hear you say). We don't know each other. A chronological A to Z would cover the interesting bits, but do conversations really develop like this? I started angling at sea. Let's start with my love affair with the sea.

It had been a long flight to Sydney Australia, via Singapore. Thankfully I can sleep on a clothes line so I wasn't too disoriented after a 24 hour flight. I remembered the days of business class travel to India with work - vibrating seats, divider between yourself and your partner. Drinks on arrival and a menu to die for. Flowers on your table and metal knives and forks. By the time you had figured out the extent of the seat permutations you had covered 5000 miles.

Guess what; I wasn't travelling business class?

I arrived at 3.00am in the morning into Sydney airport and it was deserted. Arriving at passport control, I handed my UK passport over and an eyebrow was raised. "Been here before" the man said. No was the reply. Any of your family ever visited OZ? Yeh! My Dad did during the Second World War. His aircraft carrier docked in the deep water harbour at Sydney. I felt a certain connection when he knew my family had graced the antipodean shores. It was going well until this point. I said he was locked up for being drunk and disorderly, due to drinking neaters.

Neaters I here you say. What is it?

Neaters was the rum given to the officers on board whereas the ratings got grog. Rum and water. You had to drink it daily. It wouldn't keep, but officers got the full monty. How the hell he got neaters I will never know, but he was drunk for 3 days. Even when he woke up in a police cell. He said every time you drank water it reactivated the rum. Drunk and disorderly was the charge.

He said, "well mate" in strong Queenslander accent.

"You've got a lot to live up to there".

That got me into Australia.

Just as well when he asked, "do you have a criminal record"? I had an urgent desire to say. "Do you still need one to get into OZ?" (I didn't) Now what about the fishing.

The adventure led us to Brampton Island.

It was paradise with Aussies on holiday. That meant saying no to everyone you met. No I don't want a tinny or four for a conversation. I would have been permanently pissed. I found a man who had a boat for hire. He reassured me that the sharks didn't eat you alive during the day. However, for God's sake don't go into the water at night-time.

Fishing tackle was a hand line with big blunt hooks. Blunt hooks equate to sustainable fishing. However I went along with it. The squid bait was gobbled up before it could get down to the Emperor fish that we were fishing for. The fusilier fish were well fed that day. You could see the odd barracuda swim by. Sounds bad. Nothing to worry about. Whilst paddling in the shallows, a sting ray was swimming directly towards me when it saw me. It just swam 3m around me. No interest. However, I thought, what happens if you stand on one? I followed the kangaroo footprints on the shore line. It was safer there. The sea eagle was going about its business entertaining me diving for fish. The fruit bats sounded the end of the day. Finally, keep away from the beach; the sea crocodiles don't have the same feeding time nor the same fear.

My first day fishing was with Ian Duncan, fishing off the jetty at Roker. I was 11 years old. The bus journey was epic compared to what children do today; undertake a 13 mile journey on the bus and a 3 mile walk before I started. Why is it that all the days I remember were sunny and warm? My hand line captured a small eel. That was me hooked and captured for life.

This is where a pattern started to emerge.

Friends. Fishing can be solitary, but without a friend to share it with it means nothing. How can you share a catch without sharing the landing of your catch? A decent sea fish will require two people to land it, whether it be lifting it up from the sea or netting a big river fish that once fattened itself in the sea.

Most sons will be introduced to angling by their fathers or grandfathers. However I introduced my father to sea angling. He took it up out of jealousy. I had joined Sunderland sea anglers. This meant I fished competitions with Jack Broadly who knew my father. Father was a building contractor and Jack was a building control officer. I came back with great stories of camaraderie. Jealousy got the better of him. Thank the Lord because we had some amazing days together. As I only had my father until I was 21 so the fishing days were precious.

To get me started angling, I bought a glass fibre rod from Telfers fishing tackle shop at the top of North Road in Durham. I needed a decent sea reel to go with it but could only afford a cheap river reel. A blue coloured Intrepid. My first decent fish was a mackerel but it broke the line because of the river reel line capacity when it was two feet from being landed. I could have sworn it was a barracuda. My next fish was a whiting and my Grandmother fried it for me at 2 Glue Garth, Gilesgate, where I was born. I think it has been re branded to 51 Sunderland Road.

I remember my first sizeable fish. A whiting forever etched into my memory. My grandmother cleaned and cooked it for me. A very memorable moment in my life. I also remember my first fish lost. The light line snapped whilst lifting a mackerel out of the water. Devastated was an understatement. It looked like a barracuda to me. There would be many more disappointments of this nature. Funny how angling prepares you for failure and disappointment without taking life too personally.

1966 at Seaham, Co Durham, UK

1966 saw me achieve Sunderland junior angler of the year.

Fishing Sunday competitions off Roker pier, I won the Park trophy for the heaviest junior catch of the year. It was a great year's fishing with my father. The awards ceremony was at the Locarno ballroom Sunderland. We watched cine films about fishing in Ireland and promised to fish in Ireland ourselves. I had to wait until I was 60 to fulfil this adventure. This trophy had to be returned after one Year. I was sad to see it go, however it is still in my memory. Maybe it was because there were lots of cod to catch in the North Sea at that time. How things have changed? Guess what, lots more friends. Clubs bring together like minded people that provide a framework for life. They also give you something to go back to once you have your love life in place. Angling is for life, not just for Christmas. Friends, with luck, are also friends for life, however long that is?

My dentist used to say, these teeth will last you for life! Did he know something that I didn't?

The memories I have fishing off Roker pier are mainly cold ones, frozen hands. Also the sound of black studded waders marching on concrete, was of a time. No one wears these now. They have full floatation suits. They don't know the meaning of cold?

I still love the sound of small waves breaking on a shingle beach. I have one image from the sixties that will always be with me. A moonlit night, cold, peaceful, and I found a baby seal washed up. A kind angler took it to the RSPCA. My contribution to ensuring there were less fish to catch due to the seals.

Fishing played a big part in my early teens. Some of the happiest times were through at Roker with friends. The bus journey was a big event, followed by the walk from Sunderland city centre to Roker picking up fishing bait en-route. The only bad memory I had was fishing alone when my grandfather Elliott had had a stroke, I wasn't in the best frame of mind and I threw my lead sinker into my tackle bag. The hook lodged fully into my thumb and the line and sinker wrapped itself around my neck. I was in trouble and had it not been for an off-duty ambulance driver who untangled me and kindly took me to the nearest hospital, I have no idea how I would have coped? The hospital staff were on an hour, trying to get this hook out without any anaesthetic. Quite a bad day for my parents. A father laid up with a stroke and having to collect me from hospital. I lost my granddad very soon after this. He was a very quiet man of great depth.

Preparation for fishing was a serious event. Remember the black studded waders? They were invaluable clambering across the rocks and through the rock pools when the tide was out; looking for peeler and soft back crabs for bait. Angling is a strange art. It thrives on rumour and secrets. When the word goes out all the cod will take is peeler crab, all you can fish with is peeler crab. Strange that I caught my biggest cod fishing for flatties with a strip of herring. Even stranger now we have immersed ourselves in the World of the Internet. All the cod are taking is lugworm. You try buying lugworm when this message goes viral! I believe the lugworm bait diggers association have 'plants' that distribute these 'must have' rumours to ensure a bag full of sea fish.

Preparation did not stop at finding or fishing for your own bait. There were lead weights to be made. Try getting that one past the health and safety culture of today. Handling molten lead at 11 years old. It was great fun to make a bag full of sinkers and this was satisfying in its own right but on a half crown pocket money a week. It was essential to keep the costs down.

Dad and Mam – Park Trophy for junior angler of the year

There was inspiration a plenty with Jack Hargreaves' TV program, Town and Country. In my opinion (not so humble), it has never been surpassed. A man at peace with the World, smoking his pipe in his shed. Heaven. The man wove fishing into all manner of seasons, annual events, cultural foibles, and list knowledge from the countryside. All shared with you in front of a well stoked coal fire, spitting and flickering alongside the small quiet black and white TV. Jack and the fire spoke in harmony and young minds wandered to plan their next fishing expedition. Was life any better? I can't remember it if it was. I still have a throw-back to these days with an Army surplus haversack that transported my tackle. Like most things of mine that are old, they become very precious and I hate with a vengeance the wasteful throwaway society we have today.

The teen years were spent with a fishing rod in my hand whenever the opportunity arose until I discovered the pleasures of the opposite sex. Such a lot of effort for so little reward. I should have stuck with the fishing. That's easy to say when you're in your 60s. For the next 15 years there was a lull is my piscatorial outings. I still had some memorable days fishing at Eyemouth for flatties, Sunday mornings on the Tyne estuary, with some very good natured lads from my old Polytechnic. Mackerel fishing off the cliffs at North Devon whilst young lads in a rubber dinghy hit a shark on the back with their oars. I believe this was pre "Jaws" days. What got me back into angling? I fished a pier in Virginia Beach, U.S.A. Hired a rod and caught spot and round fish. The sun was scorching hot. The locals used my fish to catch skate and shark. They say size doesn't matter. Well it did that day. However I wouldn't have missed it for a gold plated pig. The tuna fishing off Madeira was a nice day out on a boat, but that was all we caught other than the rays of the sun.

Tuna fishing off Madeira (leeward side of the island)

The biggest fish I ever saw caught on a rod and line was in the Mediterranean. It wasn't an accident. The angler had a reel big enough for tuna. I had just satisfied my hunger with seafood paella and half a bottle of the local wine. Whilst strolling along the promenade I noticed waves being created in the marina. It was only when I spotted the angler, rod bent towards the waves, that it occurred to me what might be going on. A crowd started to form around him. I had no idea what he had hooked; clearly it was a sea monster. After an hour the fish tired and came to the surface and it was a manta ray with a span of 6 feet across its back. The fish was returned to the open sea with a round of applause from the 500 people who had gathered to watch this amazing spectacle.

Pressure of running my own business required some outlet. I was already a decent club runner and was invited to run the London marathon in the early eighties. However this was not enough and the love of angling just needed a slight stoking to get the fire burning again.

Enter Lawrie Milner. An old school friend from our ice skating days. Lawrie had a passion for anything electronic and we regularly rigged up my parents' old radio set to a 100 yard long steel washing line to act as a huge aerial. He also has a passion for transmitting from an old tank radio set before he was caught red handed by the GPO. More of that from him later.

Lawrie moved in near my office and he offered me a guest ticket at Croxdale, fly fishing with his Dad. My father had bought me a Hardy Perfect fly reel for 11 guineas in the 1960s and I had never really used it. The silk line was still good so I bought a handful of small flies to fish for brown trout. The love of the silver and blue teal has never left me since I first saw these during my forays into the smoky world of Telfer's tackle shop. Telfer was a huge man and his shop was always filled with pipe smoke. A kindly man who gave me time to dream before purchasing my first fishing rod from him. However I needed a new fly rod and bought a cheap glass fibre rod to get me started again. It was a fabulous evenings fishing and I caught a very unlucky brown trout. I was like Toad of Toad Hall. Poop poop. I had gone. Little did I realise the next 27 years would be a piscatorial event.

Back to friends again. That's the difference between running and angling. Angling permits longer time for discourse. I might have caught more fish if I had spent less time talking. Talking in the car park, talking on the river bank, talking to strangers, always the best bit, talking whilst getting a bite, no wonder I don't see many wild animals, the noise must frighten them away for miles.

I started sea fishing and ended up a keen river angler.

Let's look at rivers and start with a walk along the Mississippi, which ended up at Galveston Texas on the Mexican gulf shore line.

The scale and speed of the river is unbelievable. The heat is a close second. You would have to jog to keep up with the flotsam and jetsam that are continually being swept into the Gulf of Mexico.

After saying that the view is pretty impressive. It is big enough for a 14 barge ship to make headway up the river and be a dot on the overall scale of the river. It must do 10mph to stand still, however the return journey must be very fast.

Walkers always speak when we pass, with a "how are you?"."Good" is the answer, always.

Balls of feather-like seeds are floating down all around us from the standing cottonwood riverside trees. I say standing because lining the river embankment are 100 ft long trees all aligned to the flow of the river and marooned when it dropped its level. The dead trees are bleached white with the sun and look like ghost trees. Silver maple trees disperse between the cottonwood and provide a small amount of shelter from the sun.

The smell is wonderful from a jasmine type of weed that is everywhere and it filled the hot air. In amongst the weeds fly red winged blackbirds and Citrine wagtails. Sometimes they hitch a ride on the floating trees. It is a real assault on the senses.

As a passionate angler, I wonder what monster fish live in such a massive body of fresh water. I'm guessing catfish the size of a small European car. There's nothing small around here. However the Gulf catfish are small and very good eating. You would never eat a river catfish.

Shortly after my walk along the Mississippi I visited Galveston in Texas and found the most courteous people on the planet. Southern hospitality is alive and well. The anglers I spoke to used sir as a salutation and discussed their angling tactics with great enthusiasm. I just arrived as a black tipped shark was landed. It was despatched and filleted within no time at all and placed in ice boxes to protect it from the Texan sun. This was a sharp contrast to fishing at my wet and cold homeland.

Fresh fish (fillet of shark)

Galveston – Texas

The whole of São Paulo (Brazil) live in high rise, so Sunday is the day when the whole of São Paulo go to the Ibirapuera Park. Grown men flying model aeroplanes ready for combat. They chase each other and chop off the streamers of the other plane. Watched by a tiered galley of supporters. None there when I visited but the spectator stands are testament to this. Super-fast speedboats whizzing around the boating lake until they overturn, then they are recovered with a float rod and treble hook. Noisy and exhilarating. Fishing rods are not what they seem.

Days away fishing with friends. As George Bush said, "The days a man spends fishing or spends hunting should not be deducted from the time that he's on earth", a day spent fishing is a day added onto the end of your life, not taken off it. So it was with visits to Watendlath in the Lake District. Day tickets on the Till, Teviot and Nith. If these days were measured by hope, positive feelings and anticipation then these would be the benchmark for life.

Where to start? Not the beginning (again). Watendlath. The journey is half of the day out. It used to be on a Suzuki 750 slingshot. Difficult to take all you need but the journey was nothing short of heaven on two wheels. Fishing is a peaceful sport, the journey could be less so. The red warning triangle of bends ahead created a cry of joy inside the full face helmet. Sadly the journey was over too quickly. Someone once said "breaking the rules is bad - if you get caught." Not too many speed cameras around in those days. Then came the difficult bit. Calming down sufficiently to enjoy a landscape loved by poets, painters and Herdwick sheep for hundreds of years. Thank the Lord for friends with cars who took the picnic, table, stove, fish smoker and beer. The fishing could be poor or wonderful without any link to the weather or skill. A wet day produced the biggest fish we have every caught as a team and my biggest ever at 13.5 lbs., the rainbow trout being released from a fish farm so maybe size doesn't really count in the case of stocked waters.

The best bit of every trip to Watendlath is the lunch. Two to three hours of storytelling, eating great food, often with fresh smoked fish as a starter. It always attracts visitors and they are the best part of the day as exchanging stories with strangers is wonderful. They tell you of their life and that is a joy for them to share their life with you.

Watendlath has been the starting point for fishing Dock and Blea tarns. Those days of climbing mountains to fish for fingerling brown trout seem to be a thing of the past. Maybe when I get new knee joints?

The Teviot was a treat for my 60th birthday. Fish, fish everywhere but not a one to catch. Apologies to Samuel Coleridge. The Nith was the only time I've caught a salmon in Scotland. Everyone fished the fly and after a 30 minute nap in the car, I tried a Rapala lure. I hooked into it with huge surprise as I had never caught a decent fish on a lure. The netting was something like a keystone cops scene. Shouts of "it isn't ready for the net", "net the bastard". Bloody hell what fish is ever ready to be killed? After a very snatchy fight, it was banked and duly administered the last rites. When I think of what it cost to catch one, maybe a trip to the supermarket would have made more sense? It might have, but I have a great memory. You can't take your wealth with you. The wonderful thing about catching a fish yourself is that it isn't a meal, or many meals in the case of a salmon, it is a celebration of the fish's life. As you would celebrate communion in church, I celebrate the life of one of God's creatures with the body of the fish and the finest wine I can buy to accompany the ritual. It is pagan in essence and I make no excuse for this.

Plate 6 – Teviot and friends

Shincliffe has been a refuge for the last 20 odd years.

Life has its ups and downs, but a special place in the countryside is a haven in difficult times. As soon as I pull up in the car park, under the indigenous trees, the smell of decomposing vegetation hits the nostrils and you know you've arrived. Smell is a wonderfully evocative stimulant. At Easter the smell of the bluebells fill the air, and in early June the May blossom is a subtlety fragrant scent. Let's not forget the heady fragrance of the Himalayan balsam, hated by many but loved in many circles. You know autumn is just around the corner when the balsam seeds are exploding all around. When you arrive at the river, the smell of the river takes me back to Sunday picnics at Witton le Wear Lido. Catching sticklebacks with a net. Seven years old again - some would say that's all I've ever been!

One late wet evening, I walked to the river on my own, clearly the stealth was unusual. I came across two badgers slurping slugs for supper. They were so intent on their supper that I got quite close before they saw me and they turned tail. Feeling a bit of devilment in me, I followed the Badgers' departure until one turned and let me know its disapproval. Valour left me at this point and I decided to turn tail. Probably one of my better decisions.

I can't tell you enough about how much I feel alive and part of the cosmos when sea trout fishing on a clear starlit night. Why is it anglers feel such a sense of awe at being part of nature? The better thing is that I have like-minded people to share these feelings with. It is a great reminder of our place in the Universe, especially when one get so wrapped up with day to day drudgery.

Sea trout at night – Shincliffe, Co. Durham, UK

There are three species of bats that fill the night air in summer and every now and then we catch one on the back cast. Poor buggers. Who would have thought a flying mouse could live on insects?

One warm balmy summer's evening I was getting changed at the rear of my car, squeezing myself into FB size neoprene rubber waders.

We're not going into what FB stands for. Oh, you knew; full bodied. Well done.

By chance a slender middle-aged lady approached walking her dog.

Very elegant I thought, and said hello. She asked, "Going fishing?" I don't know what came over me. "No" was the reply. "I just love the feel of rubber on skin on a warm summer's evening". That ended the conversation quite abruptly. I was on my own again. I wonder why?

This story you couldn't make up.

Later that year on a cold evening in autumn. I was wearing my neoprene waders again as a barrier against the cold. Walking with a very old mate. Yes he is very old. Ray. He went in at an easy access point of the seat pool and I ventured forth upstream another 100 yards. Old Larry would say, "When the winds in the North never venture forth", but forth I went on my own. Air temperature was about 5°C. I should have been singing "nymphs and shepherds come away, come away" etc. The Himalayan balsam and hogweed were growing to shoulder height and I went on my way through the undergrowth towards the river and down the bank side. The path was 2 ft wide and you could only see a rod length ahead. Well what happened next was nothing I could have dreamt up. Up popped a naked young lady of generous proportions. She tried to hide behind a tea towel sized towel with little success. As I said, she was of ample proportions. All points of the compass could not be covered in one. The situation required deliberation. So what does a man say where confronted by a naked young lady on a river bank?

All I could think of was, "I'm going fishing. Can I just make my way to the water?"

At this point a female head popped out from behind the voluptuous young lady and I realised she must have been smaller and thinner. One towel between them.

I asked what had happened

Remember this deliberation is taking some time, but I stood my ground. After. All, I had paid my club fees and I had a licence to fish.

They replied that they had been open water swimming!!!

I added that the water was not deep enough to swim the crawl!

They replied they did the breast stroke.

At this point I could see a headline in the local press, "University lecturer, dressed in rubber, confronts two naked women". It might have been good for my street cred at my age, however, then I thought I'd better tell my wife immediately.

I can hear you saying, this conversation is lasting a long time. Well I had a duty of care to ensure they were safe.

This 'very easy on the eye' scene terminated when one of the girls asked, "Can you give us 5 minutes to get dressed?" I replied, "Only if you shout to Ray that you were the two naked swimmers that I had stumbled across."

I left to tell a bemused Ray the tale. I could hear him thinking, "Does he think I'm as stupid as he is?" The girls saved the day and my credibility by shouting a 'hello' to Ray and to explain they had been swimming.

I did not catch a fish that night, but who the hell cares.

Succession planning

Who will inherit my fishing tackle? I still have my father's fishing tackle, my grandfather's lawn mower, so there is my Hardy split cane fly rod and Hardy Perfect fly reel to find a home for. I find the longer you have a possession, the more valuable it becomes. Patrick, my grandson, was taken to Hury reservoir at the age of five. A beautiful sunny day and one small rainbow trout to take home. He was as hooked as I was forty years earlier. He has fished Watendlath with the men, which he loved, and to this day still lives for his coarse and sea fishing. He has made friends with another angler, so that's him set for life. Thankfully I'm still allowed to take him for days out. My fishing days are not over yet!

Some Other People's Lives

Hury reservoir and Patrick

An Offer of Marriage

by Geoff O'Brien

In 1981 I was sent to Thailand. I was then employed in the oil exploration business and had lived and worked in a number of places prior to being sent to Thailand. It is a wonderful country with warm and friendly people. It is a land of temples, Bhuddas, klongs (canals), paddy fields and great food. Thai restaurants have the biggest menus I have ever seen and their cuisine seems to be a fusion of different styles of Asian cooking.

After landing at Bangkok airport I transferred to a local flight to a place called Khon Kaen where the crew was based. Khon Kaen is sort of in the middle of Thailand and we intended to survey up to the border with Laos. Wherever we could we would survey along road but there were many times we worked off-road. The area around Khon Kaen was dominated by agriculture. Unsurprisingly the main crop was rice. Though the landscape was dominated by paddies there were stands of trees and lots of small villages with houses built on stilts. Every house seemed to have chickens, ducks and pigs and what appeared to be a kitchen garden. Every now and then we would see a monk leading a line of young men with shaven heads and dressed in saffron robes and carrying begging bowls. It is customary and regarded as part of their education for young men to spend one year in the monastery. The Thais take their religion very seriously and I observed the generosity of what were quite poor people. But that is often the case.

When I arrived the rainy season was over and the rice was beginning to grow and the paddies were still filled with water. It was hot and humid. One day some of the crew caught a fish in one of the klongs that fed water to the paddies. The crew always seemed to be on the outlook for something to eat. We did feed them really well but the crew liked to stop fairly frequently for a snack. Anyway, in no time at all they started a fire, a pan miraculously appeared filled with water from the Klong and was put on the fire to boil. Then a number of the crew seemed to go foraging. "What are they looking for?" I asked Dang my driver/translator. "They look for some flavours. Fish have little taste and needs to be spiced." When they arrived back the fish has just began to boil. Handfuls of greens were thrown in along with a handful of ants. "Why ants?" I asked. "Gives flavour like lemon" I was told. They were right! The fish was delicious!

On another day I saw two men with blowpipes. I asked my Dang to find out what they were hunting. He told they were going to a stand of trees to hunt for lizards that the local people prize as a delicacy. But I diverge I hear you say. This is supposed to be about an offer of marriage! As I said earlier we often worked off-road. That meant that we had to cross land belonging to the local villages. In order to get permission we sent scouts ahead to meet with the village headman. We would pay for access and compensation for any damage we might cause. One day around lunchtime Dang drove up to where I was working with the crew. He told me that a local headman wanted to meet me. I asked if this was about money or compensation. No I was told. He wanted to meet me as he had never met a foreigner or 'Falang' in Thai. I agreed to this as it is not a good idea to say no to a headman!

We drove as near to the village as we could. I grabbed a water bottle and a few packs of cigarettes - I used to smoke in those days - and we set off for the village. At first sight the village seemed like many of the others in the area; a group of wooden buildings on stilts with livestock and gardens. There was one difference. The houses were built around a platform. The platform was covered with dried palm fronds and sitting on this was a man. He was dressed in a sarong and wore what looked like local jewellery around his neck. His face and body were sculpted; no doubt from working in the paddies. He was really a very handsome man and definitely had a presence. He was quite young - around the same age as me. I was in my late twenties at that time. Sitting behind him in a semi-circle is what appeared to be the whole village. I asked Dang to introduce me. I walked towards him and bowed. He bowed back. I offered my hand while Dang explained that it is a Falang custom to shake hands when meeting someone for the first time. We did so. He then offered me a cigarette. Local Thai cigarettes are made from coarse tobacco rolled in something that resembles newspaper. I offered him a Marlboro. He gestured for me to sit. We lit our cigarettes.

I asked Dang to thank the headman for the invitation and say that I was very honoured. There was some exchange between them and then Dang went up to the headman and whispered in his ear. The headman announced what I had said to the villagers. There were some Oohs and Aahs. I then realised what had happened. The headman would relay our conversation to the villagers. This was clearly a man who wanted control over the message to his villagers. So that is how our conversation continued. I was asked a question. Dang translated in English, I answered, Dang whispered the translation to the headman and he announced it to the villagers.

What sort of things was I asked about? I was asked a great many different things. Where did I come from and how did I get here. I told him where I came from and that I had flown to Thailand. I pointed upwards. The headman said that he had seen these things in the sky. He asked what it was like to fly. I tried my best to explain. I sensed that few had travelled much beyond the village. He then asked me about England. He had never heard of it and asked if it was far away from here. I said it was many thousands of miles and Dang seemed to translate this in a way that the headman understood and when he announced it to the villagers there were gasps of disbelief. He then asked about our houses and what kind of rice we grew. I told him we lived in brick houses. We had some problems with the concept of bricks but managed to overcome that by saying it was like dried clay. When I told him that we did not grow rice, all were astonished. I explained about our climate and that we grew different types of crops such as wheat and barley. After a few rounds of this I clearly managed to convey that the lifestyle in England was very different from here.

The headman then asked me what I was doing here. I tried my best to explain that we were looking for oil and gas by saying we were searching for paraffin and kerosene. These are used quite extensively and so I think I conveyed successfully what I was doing. Then came the personal questions; how old was I? Was I married? When I said no that caused quite a stir amongst the villagers. I could not see what was happening but there appeared to be quite a bit of movement and the headman seemed to be giving directions. He then spoke.

"Your country and your way of life are very different to ours. Your houses are different and you grow different crops and your food will not be the same as ours."

He clapped his hand and six girls dressed traditionally and with their faces painted white entered the circle and stood before the platform. There was much nervous giggling and they all tried to avoid the eyes of the headman. A white face is a sign of great beauty and wealth as you do not have to work in the sun. The headman spoke again.

"You can have one of these as your wife. You can take her to your country and she can learn your ways. She can also teach your people our ways. Your children will know of both worlds and this will bring us closer together and make for a better place."

I was overwhelmed. I did realise that this was a very tricky situation and I had to find a way out of this in such a way that the headman did not lose face with his villagers. I offered a cigarette and we smoked. I believed that the headman was sincere and far sighted. His offer was well intended and it would have been a grave insult to refuse it out of hand. Headmen are quite powerful figures amongst their villagers and this needed to be handled with care.

I thanked him profusely for his generosity. I said I was astonished at seeing so many beautiful girls. And they really were beautiful! I said he must be very proud to be the headman of a village that had so many beautiful girls. I then told him that my job was like being in the military. He seemed to understand that. We were not allowed wives. I told him that we also moved around a lot and I never knew where I was going next. Even if I could marry then I would not be able to spend much time with her as I was constantly on the move. She would be very lonely. Yes I did tell a few little white lies but, I thought appropriate at the time. I spent almost an hour trying to wriggle away from this situation and, as the headman spoke my words to the villagers, I sensed that some understanding of my predicament was emerging. He asked how long I would stay in the job. I said two more years. He then said, "come here then and choose a wife." I said I was deeply honoured and would do all I could to return. After many farewells I left with Dang. I realised when I returned to the camp that I had not asked his name. Whoever he was he was certainly an extraordinary man.

Brushes with Death (A Painter's Story)

by Francis Henry Pylon (This article was sponsored by Bring Out Your Dead Burial services – fast to despatch)

To paraphrase Oscar Wilde, "To have one accident is unfortunate, to have two is careless". How many lives do you have in one lifetime? Looking back at many brushes with death, it's surprising for me to be writing this!

Chronologically, at the age of four, I was hit by a car and sent flying down and across the main road outside my house. I have no knowledge of this and it hasn't left me with any visible impairment. Honest. After reading this you may think otherwise.

The road on which I came into to contact with a moving vehicle had four cars a day going along it. How unlucky can you be? The village only had two cars, ours and the shop owners. There were regular bus services but I didn't get hit by a bus (that nearly happened whilst cycling 40 years later). It was a car. Now keep up!

My village reminds me (loosely) of the green lanes in Eire: little traffic and Geordie on his holidays with his trouble and strife and only two children because he wasn't a good "upstanding" Catholic. "Upstanding" Catholics have many more children. Well moving on!

Geordie was having his shipyard fortnight break in Southern Ireland. He had found a liking for Guinness in the local tavern. This left the wife and children safely at home in the best North East tradition of misogyny. His love of the local camaraderie and Guinness built during his first week of the holiday, until at last orders he shouted loudly, "bugger the Pope".

When he awoke in hospital surrounded by his family, he asked what had caused this event? His long suffering wife explained that in Southern Ireland there is a strong catholic presence. They worship the Pope and any insult will result in this hospitalisation or death. She went on to explain that in the "troubles", Catholics shot Protestants and Protestants shot Catholics. She advised that religion in general was best avoided and in particular your own preference should definitely not be revealed to anyone who might ask.

Geordie revisited the pub where the altercation had taken place. He bought everyone a drink and unreservedly apologised for his callous actions. This time at last orders he wished them well and left feeling pretty good with the outcome. He stumbled out into the moonlight - leprechauns were leaping in the distant mist as he returned to his holiday caravan and his family.

His feet had lost their compass but he managed a tortuous route towards home, when out of the bushes leapt two hooded would be assassins, dressed in battle fatigues, and full face balaclava woollen helmets only showed their steely eyes.

They shouted to Geordie, "What religion are you"?

Geordie's blood ran cold, the banshee wailed overhead and Darby O'Gill sat puffing his pipe, on a stone milestone to Dublin, awaiting the outcome of this heist. He remembered his wife's wise words: "Catholics shoot Protestants and Protestants shoot Catholics". She advised that religion in general was best avoided and in particular your own preference should definitely not be revealed." Geordie was no fool, he shouted loudly and confidently, "I'm Jewish", and they opened up with their AK 47s and blew him to bits. When they removed their balaclavas and congratulated each other, the comment was made – "We must be the luckiest Arabs in Ireland."

At this point in the tale I could recount the Irishman whom I nearly killed on my motorbike, but I'll save that until later - so moving on.

Let's take a trip back to my village in the 1950s. The summers were long, dry and dusty, and over the fields, known as the Scrambles, National motorcycling scrambling events were held, featuring machines by Greeves, BSA, Ariel, Vincent, AJS, Norton, Matchless, Enfield and James. Where are they now? The leaking of oil was de rigueur, colour schemes were black and chrome, and among the competitors were famous names of the day. However a BSA Gold Star tank badge was a thing of real beauty if the only splendid bit of the bike, as BSA stood for "bastard stopped again", or was it British Small Arms? I could still be tempted to ride a BSA 650 Rocket, if only I could figure out how to start it? Kick start with a decompression lever and manual timing advance, oh boy, difficult.

Bikes parked in the sun, leaking oil at Belmont scrambles, they were lined along the roadside and there was a heady smell of oil and petrol. These were treasured memories of beauty. This is where my lifelong love of motorcycles started. It hasn't waned since my first shared ownership of a James 197 motorcycle in 1966 that was powered with a Villiers engine.

I remember emulating my scrambling heroes on a bicycle and going down sections of the Scrambles track at breakneck speed until we were catapulted over the handlebars and landed in a heap 20 metres from whence we parted company from our wrecked Raleigh bike. Strangely enough, we never broke any bones! The bike didn't fare as well. Young lads ain't fearless, they just don't know when to back off; however, I'm still here to tell the tale.

My sixteenth birthday arrived, and with it a second hand police Vespa scooter. It is ironic that a great big size 12 flat foot policeman should have the indignity of riding an under powered Italian gadabout, designed for Rome and used with flip flops. The Vespa was police blue and it had had a radio set on the pillion space. It wasn't long before I bought a BSA Rocket style seat for my scooter, along with the statutory back rest. Falling off a Vespa was never difficult. I found lots of Tarmac to acquaint myself with. The worst falling off was at low speed, when the clutch lever embedded itself in my leg. My most memorable 50 mph dismount happened at the bottom of a hill when the suspension bottomed out. I was off in the blink of an eye and sliding along head first with my crash helmet acting as a brake to slow me down, between road and kerb. The helmet looked like a curly perm by the time I had finished with it. The throttle had stuck on full and the screaming and wailing banshee was 50m from me. All I had to do was face the indignity of falling off and go back to switch it off. That was when I realised I had fallen due to black ice, I couldn't stand up, and a Vaux beer tanker was sliding out of control towards me as I lay in the middle of the road trying to recover my breath from a heavy landing and bouncing around. My flying jacket took the brunt of the impact, but I wasn't ready to stand up, and this tanker, now sideways, was about to end my life. All I could think of was, "killed by a Vaux tanker". It wasn't decent beer in my opinion. Needless to say it missed me, otherwise I wouldn't be writing this today

I was 19 years old and part of the CITB training scheme. I had an appointment at 10am with the supervisor of the scheme. Little did I know that thirty years later I would have another supervisor to conclude my education. Really it isn't a conclusion, but the completion of an apprenticeship that permits access to a different life in research.

The family business was dependent upon reliable labour and this was Monday morning. Reliable labour did not include a night at the Working Men's club and the subsequent inebriation. So, Davy was absent and I was sent to collect him or find out what had caused his failure to put in an appearance with the rest of the workmen. I was given the bosses car, which was a six cylinder 3 litre Ford Zodiac. It was a beast of a car designed in the style of an American Cadillac without the wings on the back. It bounced in every conceivable direction when under a fullness of steam, and as I was going to be late for my CITB appointment I floored it! A new housing estate was being constructed and the site entrance was between two villages of Broom Park and Ushaw Moor in County Durham. As I overtook two sixteen wheeler Foden wagons parked opposite the gap in the hedge, a Commer wagon pulled out blocking the road in front of me. Oh shit, I thought. Little did I know I would utter the same comments 26 years later but end up in a much worse condition. I hit the brakes on a muddy road and slid into the Foden wagons. I remember the bang and the car pole vaulted into the air, at which point I jumped out, only to find I was in mid air. I kicked the door closed and landed heavily on the road on my back. What direction you land in determines what you observe. I observed the underside of the car coming down onto me. Thankfully the Commer wagon was an old fashioned type with a bonnet and the rear of the car landed on the bonnet. As it hit the wagon I was showered with red hot pieces of rust. Then a building site labourer grasped me firmly and lifted me from under the car. The car was a total write-off and the police couldn't understand how I got out as the doors were jammed solid. All I suffered was a minor cut to my left arm as I raised it to protect my head from the impact. I was not wearing a seat belt, as had I been wearing one I would have been trapped inside the car. All I got from my father when the ambulance took me home was, "I put a new exhaust on it. I can see you are all alright." That was the sympathy I got from a man who had witnessed a young officer cut in two, having been in the unfortunate position of standing on a join on an aircraft carrier deck when a Japanese kamikaze pilot flew into the deck. The plates parted and the officer fell through, and when they snapped back, he was cut cleanly in two. The Torso (white tropical uniform and sun tan) was on deck, and other half was below the flight deck. He told me, "you don't die instantly as in the films." What a thing to have to live with. No wonder he could see objectively that I was ok.

My entry into the big bike world with a Honda K7 was a shock to the system. I had the bike delivered to give me time to get used to this awesome power and weight. Excited about my new second hand purchase which I bought with money left to me by a great aunt, I set off from home very gingerly.

The bikes had petrol taps fitted in those days and this day the petrol tap was the harbinger of my demise. I was travelling very carefully towards Shincliffe and a right turn was required, so I tipped it into a slow right hand corner when the bike cut out as I hadn't switched the petrol tap on, and home to Sherburn House was the distance the bike went until the fuel ran out. Precisely in the middle of a corner!!! "Oh bugger". The bike leant over and kept going over because there was no power to straighten it up. I ended up trapped under nearly a quarter of a ton of metal and not one bastard car driver stopped to help me out. They all drove around me whilst I was pinned onto the road by the bike. Needless to say I survived but maybe I should have looked before I leapt? I learned from this and never repeated my mistake.

The arrival at Douglas on the Isle of Man was greeted by a beer fuelled festival of rock music, laughter and Castrol R. My first lap of the mountain circuit was tiptoeing around the bendy bits, until I came upon a phalanx of Manx Nortons and Tritons, all running on Castrol R and all with megaphone exhaust that made a noise like all hell breaking loose. I knew my bike was a lot faster than their classics, however, when I followed these old guys, I realised that they were very quick through the bends. I followed them up to a bend and they all left me until I caught them on the straight. This happened many times before I trusted their judgement. This was it, I was going to tip it in to a left hand bend at their speed. A warning board and straw bales signalled the corner's approach. That is nonsense as the corner didn't approach. I approached it. My heart still trembles at the prospect. It was like following a pack of dominos falling down. The first one flipped over, then the second and so on until it was my turn. Bugger it, I went for it and came out the other side flying. A truly amazing experience! Not one of them touched their brakes, which is the sign of a man in control, or woman, as I was to find out! However, if someone had 'dropped it' you would hit them, as you committed to a racing line and had to trust it. My logic said there were too many variables out there to do this with confidence. Bollocks; it was exciting and I wasn't going to miss this despite the danger!

The nearest I came to coming a real cropper was in 1982 on the Isle of Man TT circuit, after the racing on the Saturday. I knew I was going to ride fast because I put on extra layers of padding - just in case! However, coming into Ballugh Bridge, I was passed by a very shapely bottom in pale blue leathers. That was it. I had to keep up with her because my manhood was at stake. Or was it steak? She had a faster bike than my ageing Honda, despite the fact that I had souped it up with a Yoshimura exhaust and Rickman fairing that afforded me an extra 15 mph. I gave no thought to improving the rest of the bike. Just the top speed and handling. I'm sure changing the brake fluid and improving the brakes should have been a priority. I didn't care, speed was king. I nearly had a head-on crash at the Ramsey hairpin. I had flogged that Honda for all it was worth out of Parliament Square in Ramsey and I didn't realise that the brake fluid was beginning to boil as I overshot the braking zone before tipping it in around the left handed hairpin. I laid it over as far as I dared then met the wild eyed stare from a biker doing exactly the same into the hairpin as a right handed turn. Our wild eyed stares met going head on for each other at the Ramsey hairpin. All I could do was lean the bike far enough over so that everything decked out. That was all I could do. The other biker, however, had to straighten it up to avoid me. The result was that the other biker careered through a hedge to join the bits of sidecar from a previous crash. Needless to say I never stopped but just kept going on my adrenalin fuelled lap. I had no idea what was to come next. The rest was terrifying to a man who understands his mortality. Roads that would catapult you through the air if you got it wrong over the mountain. Tramlines with no grip as we hurtled over the veranda. After an off and on brake section that the real racers go flat out through, I arrived at the descent to Creg ny Baa. Adrenalin was in charge of my mind and the throttle was held wide open during the descent. 130 mph at least with a 50 mph right hander at the bottom. The crowd on the terraces at the Creg was similar to a premier league football match. I tried the front brake, as at that speed the back brake is worse than useless and throws you off. The lever came back to the bar with no pressure whatsoever. I remember this very clearly. Oh shit. 130 mph into a 50 mph corner, 60 mph if I was feeling very brave. I touched the cable operated back brake but that just unsteadied me without any slowing affect. As I approached what I thought was a certain crash, I saw a gate, off the slip road. What the hell; I went for it. Now things happen very quickly at this speed. I shot through the gate onto a gravel pathway. I tried the brakes to no effect and still doing over 100mph realised I couldn't hit them hard for fear of falling off. In the distance there was I hedge that I was expecting to launch myself over.

However, the brake fluid was starting to cool and the brakes were starting to work. Then I believed there was a God; I found 100m of Tarmac path before the hedge and obligatory ditch in front of it. Still travelling at 70 mph I hit the front brake hard on the Tarmac, the speedo going to zero, because the wheel was locking up, the back wheel skipping in the air and I stopped within half a metre of the ditch and hedge.

Time to check my underpants!

Turning the bike around proved difficult as I was trembling so much. I rode slowly back to the Creg pub to a standing ovation from the drunk spectators. I didn't stop to acknowledge the fact I had nearly been a sad statistic. Embarrassment was as bad as the fear of meeting the reaper at Creg ny Baa. I rode back to Douglas at a stately pace (stately with the odd foot peg scraping the road) compared to earlier in the day. I did a lap at about half the speed of the racers of the day or twice as long in terms of time. How do they ride so fast and stay in control?

A Manx hotelier, whom I got to know quite well as chairman of the Chartered Institute of Building in the North East of England, related a story of an all-night drinking session at which, at four in the morning, bravado reached a peak and a very drunk average motorcyclist stated he could do a 20 minute lap, which is suicidally quick. He left at Four a.m. and the drinking party expected to hear from the hospital or worse when he arrived back doing a sub 30 minute lap. How? We will never know.

That's where I went wrong. I was sober. I should have been pissed, it would have been easier.

It was 1983 and I had just bought a brand new Kawasaki 1100 motorcycle. It was at the time the fastest road bike available, until Kawasaki brought out the 900 which was water cooled and smaller, and which went faster. Well at least I had six months of owning one of the fastest road bikes in the World. It was an attention grabber at the time. Bright red with black chromed exhaust pipes. Brum brum, I was in love.

I gave an old mate Pat Dougherty a ride on the back to let him experience the silky smooth power. Pat had a mate called Pat who was into drinking rather heavily at the time. Both Irish, and is everyone called Pat I hear you asking?

I called for a pint at my local, a single drink before I went home. That was when the 'troubles' kicked off. Pat demanded a ride in my new bike to experience the at-oneness and zen-like experience of travelling together in harmony with the law of physics, in balance and flowing like a bird through the air. Little did I know that Pat could fly, but more of that later. He was now getting stroppy and I thought, he's a big lad, I'm not - go on then, but just 100 m up the road and off, however, it was a cool evening and I advised him to put his jacket on back to front to keep the wind out.

My last words to him were, "Now hang on tight." Tight is a concept better understood if you are sober, secondly, if you have any idea why you need to hang on and what forces you expect to encounter. So, I blipped the throttle up to 40 mph in first. I heard this, "arrrhhhh", felt nails dig in my neck as Pat tried to hang on, and saw a pair of heels shoot past my head as he flew backward through the air. When I turned around, I saw a crowd starting to gather around the pile on the road that was once my old mate Pat. Bugger I thought, I've killed him. The gathering crowd could see the sorry state he was in, with skin missing all over his back. I asked, "Are you alright?" He replied, "I was, until those bastards tried to turn my head around to match my jacket."

Now you must ask yourself, is this an Irish tall tale? Or is it largely the truth? I'll leave you to decide as it still makes me feel uncomfortable to this day and the good news is that we are still good mates.

It was a beautiful sunny day and I wanted to watch the motorcycling racing at Oliver's Mount at Scarborough. I had recently settled in with a new partner and got on very well with her two girls. Helen was the youngest of the two and she volunteered to ride pillion to Scarborough with me. We made rapid progress on my Suzuki 750 slingshot, weaving our way past cars and bikes, until I came up behind a Ducati SS using Castrol R oil. With the warm sun on my black leathered back and the smell of Castrol R coming from the Duke, I wasn't going to overtake no matter how slowly he rode. What an assault on the senses Castrol R is. It is the most lovely smell in the World, coupled with the pop, pop of the Duke, it was like bathing in a hot tub whilst smelling roses and listening to a Beethoven symphony. The racing was good to watch as Barry Sheene was racing, however, after it finished, I abandoned Helen for a race back home with the lads. This is when I had a cathartic moment. I realised at 150mph on a country road that my mates were pulling away from me. It was time to stop as it was becoming too dangerous. Little did I know that cycling would inflict a far heavier price in terms of injury. The motorbike was stolen and times were hard financially, so I took up cycling to protect my knees from the pounding they had received by running marathons, and entered the world as a cyclist. All was going well towards my first 100 mile cycling day out when an old codger in a car hit me in Durham's city centre. I was catapulted into the path of a bus coming towards me. It just missed me, but I actually saw stars and couldn't move. My left arm and shoulder had been broken into five pieces. It was ironic that I should stop motorcycling because it was becoming too dangerous only to be wiped out by an old codger in a flat cap whom I could hear arguing with a bystander that it was my fault for running into him. The magistrates thankfully disagreed with his logic or lack of it. Six months later I could return to work after a six hour operation and daily physiotherapy. So when finances got better I went out and bought another motorbike. I thought what the hell! Life is just a lottery!

Life threatening accidents tend to be in your own hands. Very much a behavioural thing. The accident of being in the wrong place at the wrong time comes to mind with this concluding tale. The tales starts with a bar re-fitting that went very well. Little did anyone know how it would turn out!

The scenario is a local hotel. I remember the manager as a florid overweight man who never got out of his dressing gown. His wife on the other hand was stunning and very fit.

Enter the protagonist. A fine looking blond haired young man who could sing to please the ladies and could break three pieces of 9" x 2" soft wood simultaneously with two fists and one foot. This was carried out by standing on one foot and breaking the timber. It was a truly horrifying display of power. He was a fourth Dan karate expert who could hang a door pretty well.

So!!! We were fitting a bar out at a local hotel. The manager was very pleased with our efforts and he put on a free bar for the workmen.

Exit right common sense.

Enter left the good looking joiner and the manager's wife.

Good looking joiner decided she wanted his body there and then.

Funny, because he would never have done this sober.

The old flirtatious scenario developed. Manager objected at the attention his wife was receiving from the joiner. Joiner got stroppy and the police were called. The first contingent of police to arrive were flattened by the joiner and a van full of policemen were called to cover the situation. It took twelve of them to subdue the joiner and that's when I got the call from the police station to say they had one of our employees in custody.

This is where wrong place at the wrong time comes into play.

My father, who ran the business, asked me if I would mind delivering the P45. He had had multiple heart attacks and was in no condition to endure the stress from delivering a P45 to a potential killing machine I said OK, and as I drove to the joiner's home I thought; the sun looked good, the green fields looked even better. Was this the last of my England I was about to experience? This could be my last journey in life?

I arrived to find the braced, ledged and framed door was in matchstick pieces in the yard. No mean feat by anyone with a sledge hammer, however this was carried out with fists and a huge amount of anger.

The ex-employee stood in the doorway and reassured me that I was in no danger. I must have looked as if I needed the reassurance from the wide eyed stare and trembling hand. It was no time for me to be brave, this wasn't going to be Daniel in the lion's den.

Alcohol is a strange beast as William Shakespeare alluded to in Macbeth. The conversation between the porter whilst conversing with Macduff, went like this.

Drink, sir, is a great provoker of three things.

What three things does drink especially provoke?

Marry, sir, nose-painting, sleep, and urine. Lechery, sir, it provokes, and un-provokes; it provokes the desire, but it takes away the performance: therefore, much drink may be said to be an equivocator with lechery: it makes him, and it mars him; it sets him on, and it takes him off; it persuades him, and disheartens him; makes him stand to, and not stand to; in conclusion, equivocates him in a sleep, and, giving him the lie, leaves him.

I had arrived at the home of our joiner in the despairing phase of alcohol where, if he viewed himself, the face in the mirror was a sallow guilty and remorseful one. The waning of the alcohol proved to be my saviour. The wages were made up along with the P45 and we lost a very good craftsman to lechery and alcohol.

And finally.

Nothing could be less life threatening than angling. Some call it fishing, but as old Larry used to say, that's with boats, trawlers, drifters etc. A piscatorial life is spent dreaming of what might be. Catches to be caught, dreams to be fulfilled. Liaisons to be had - and fantasies coming true. Was it the reality of being slow to strike into a bite and set the hook because we know we have to do this to be catching salmon, or was it daydreaming about the belle de jour that made our reactions slow. I guess it was belle de jour?

My old mate Paul Winstanley fell off a pier in New Zealand, hit his head on the way down and drowned. Angling was pretty terminal in his case. I wonder what he was dreaming of at the time of his piscatorial passing?

I was fishing at Roker jetty and was in one of those teenage moods, where I wasn't sure if I should go fishing or not. I caught nothing after a full day's fishing, and out of frustration and teenage belligerence, I threw the 6 oz. lead weight sinker with a stainless steel 3/0 hook attached at my haversack. The hook embedded itself into my thumb and the sinker and line wrapped itself around my neck, about six times. I couldn't get it off with my free right hand. I was starting to turn blue due to strangulation.

At this point an off-duty ambulance driver untangled me and allowed me to breathe normally. I spent 4 hours in A & E whilst the nurses tried tin snips to cut a stainless steel hook that was completely through my thumb. All that happened was that the snips twisted the hook in my thumb and I cringed in pain. This happened many times before they gave up. They eventually cut the point off the hook to pull it out against the barbs that kept the bait on, but I had had enough at this point and just suffered in silence. I was collected by both my parents who had been attending to my Granddad; the Germans didn't shoot this Durham Light Infantryman but a stroke got him nonetheless. It rounded off a perfectly awful day. Thank the Lord there are more good ones than bad.

To sum up this 'dance macabre' in a Shakespearian vein:

"Life ... is a tale. Told by an idiot, full of sound and fury. Signifying nothing."

Printed in Great Britain
by Amazon.co.uk, Ltd.,
Marston Gate.